MARY FORD

Making
GLOVE
PUPPETS

With step-by-step instructions

ACKNOWLEDGEMENTS

MARY FORD acknowledges with grateful thanks the work of Anne Sexton in designing and making the puppets used in this book. Also the contribution of her husband, Michael Ford, who in addition to being editor of the book, took all the photographs.

AUTHORS

MARY FORD'S highly successful series of cake artistry books is well known. She has had a life-long interest in all crafts and in this book she once again collaborates with toy-maker Anne Sexton to produce an entirely new range of puppets.

ANNE SEXTON is a professional toy-maker with a reputation for quality and inventive designs. She made puppets to amuse her own children when they were young and then turned her hobby into a successful career. She now exhibits extensively at Craft Fairs throughout the South of England but her toys are exported all over the world.

OTHER MARY FORD TITLES

101 CAKE DESIGNS
ANOTHER 101 CAKE DESIGNS
CONCISE BOOK OF CAKE MAKING AND
   DECORATING
MAKING CAKES FOR MONEY
SUGAR FLOWERS CAKE DECORATING
A CAKE FOR ALL SEASONS
MAKING SOFT TOYS
SUGARPASTE CAKE DECORATING
WRITING IN ICING
CHOCOLATE COOKBOOK
PARTY CAKES

Copyright 1991 Mary Ford Publications Limited.

Published by Mary Ford Publications Limited,
294b Lymington Road, Highcliffe-on-Sea, Christchurch BH23 5ET.

ISBN 0 946429 2 6 X

Printed and bound in Hong Kong

Contents

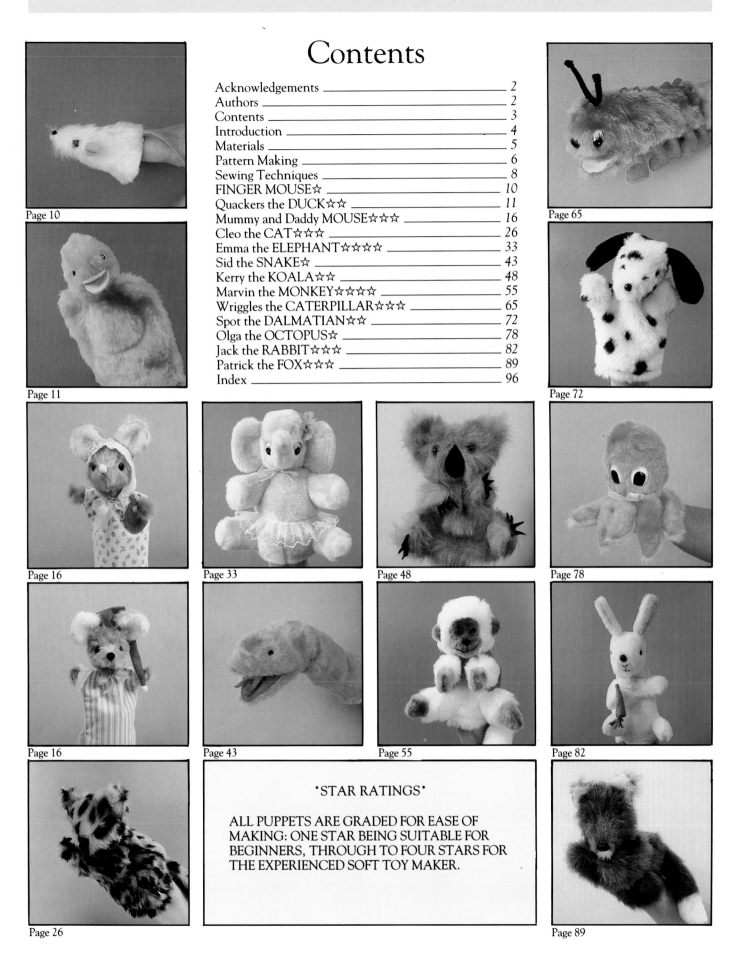

Page 10

Page 11

Page 65

Page 72

Page 16

Page 33

Page 48

Page 78

Page 16

Page 43

Page 55

Page 82

Page 26

STAR RATINGS

ALL PUPPETS ARE GRADED FOR EASE OF
MAKING: ONE STAR BEING SUITABLE FOR
BEGINNERS, THROUGH TO FOUR STARS FOR
THE EXPERIENCED SOFT TOY MAKER.

Page 89

Introduction

This is the second in my series of step-by-step Soft Toy Books and I hope it will bring to you as much pleasure as my first book — MAKING SOFT TOYS.

In this new book I have once again worked closely with Anne Sexton to produce a wide range of colourful hand, finger, long-arm and full-bodied puppets to delight children of all ages. Full-size cutting templates are included for each puppet together with a structured, step-by-step photographic guide to making up. Every completed puppet is beautifully illustrated with a large format full-colour photograph. Each puppet is carefully graded for the degree of difficulty involved and the puppets are equally suited to the experienced needlewoman (four stars) or those who are just beginning this rewarding hobby (one star).

The finished puppets are lively and exciting and have been designed to stimulate a young child's imagination and to facilitate the development of physical dexterity. They both educate and amuse, encouraging children to explore an inner world of fantasy and the outer world around them. Educationalists have long recognised the value of play in helping children to understand and integrate events and emotions into their experience of life. I am sure that the fourteen puppets in this new book will quickly become treasured friends and companions.

Mary Ford

Materials

To ensure durability of the finished puppets, the best quality and most appropriate materials should be used. The appeal of a puppet can be considerably enhanced by the imaginative selection of colour and texture.

When purchasing materials ensure that they comply with the statutory regulations for children's toy materials.

NOTE: *For photographic purposes, a contrasting thread has been used to show the stitching line. However, a matching or toning thread should always be used for sewing the puppets.*

FUR FABRIC
A fur fabric with a supple knitted backing is ideal for puppets as it stretches slightly and does not fray. A good quality fur has dense pile through which the backing is not visible — when a hand is run against the pile, the backing material should not show through.

○ **Polished fur** has a short, shiny pile.
○ **Plush fur** has a thick, shorter pile.
○ **Super soft pile fur** has a longer, dense pile.
○ **Long haired fur** has long, polished pile.
○ **'Special Furs' include** Leopard and Dalmatian.

FELT
Felt can be purchased in a wide range of colours in small squares or from the roll. Polyester felt is not a strong fabric, but it is washable and can be used for lining ears or making feet and beaks.

LINING
Suitable soft material should be used for linings and clothes.

FILLING
Hi Loft polyester filling is recommended as it is washable, springy and non-allergic. Foam chips should not be used as tiny pieces of foam can easily be inhaled by small children.

Tools

The right tool for the job is essential. Gather together all materials and tools prior to cutting and sewing as this makes the work much quicker and easier. Most of the tools required are contained in a dressmaker's kit and all the puppets in this book were made using an ordinary domestic sewing machine.

SCISSORS
A good, sharp pair of scissors is required for cutting fabric. An old pair of scissors should be used for pattern and template cutting. A small, pointed pair of embroidery scissors is also useful.

PAPER AND CARD
Tracing paper should be used for tracing templates, which are then transferred to durable card. A thin coat of latex fabric adhesive can be used to glue tracing paper to card.

PENS AND PENCILS
A felt tip pen can be used for tracing or drawing on card but should not be used on fabric. A 2B lead pencil is suitable for marking light coloured fabrics and dressmaker's chalk for darker fabrics.

PINS AND NEEDLES
Pins and needles should be counted before and after use. Extra long pins with a coloured bead head should be used. Medium needles are required for hand-sewing and a darning needle for sewing on heads and embroidery. No.16 or 18 machine needles are the most durable.

STUFFING TOOLS
Most shapes can be stuffed by hand but a screwdriver, unsharpened pencil or the blunt end of a knitting needle can be used for small work.

BRUSHES
A teazle brush is required to bring up the pile of fur fabric after handling or sewing and a clothes brush for brushing the finished puppet.

Pattern Making

TEMPLATES

The templates in this book are all full size and ready for the preparation of a pattern on card, as shown pictorially in steps 1-9 below. 'Spot the Dalmatian' is used here as an example but the principle is the same for all pattern making. Always ensure that all markings, instructions, etc., are transferred from each template in the book to the pattern.

NOTE: *Due to restrictions on space, some templates are shown drawn inside another one. Each one should be traced onto a separate sheet. Do not cut out smaller template from inside a larger one.*

KEY TO PATTERN MARKINGS	
Cutting line	———
Joining line	∼∼∼
Stitching line	— — —
Fold line	– – – –
Direction of pile or straight of fabric	⟹
Position of eye	●
Position of ears or tail	=
Easing or snipping points	◄

A clearly labelled paper bag or envelope should be used to store the completed pattern.

PATTERN LAYOUT

Having made the pattern, select an appropriate piece of material and, if using fur fabric, check the direction of the pile by running the flat of the hand across the pile. In one direction the pile will be raised up from the surface of the fabric, in the other it will lie smooth. Turn the fabric over, pile side to the table, and mark with an arrow the direction in which the fabric lies smoothly. (On smooth fabric mark the straight of the fabric.) The fabric should be placed on the table so that the pile is lying smoothly towards you. The puppet will then appear to 'stand up' as the patterns are laid out. Do not use the selvedge edge. Match the arrows on the pattern to the arrow indicating pile direction on the fabric so that patterns all lie in the same direction. Position the larger pieces first and then the smaller pieces can be fitted in, remembering to check the direction of the pile. Ensure that all patterns are correctly positioned and that no piece has been omitted.

Draw around all the patterns, marking light coloured fabric with soft lead pencil and dark fabric with chalk (this is the cutting line). Carefully cut around each pattern with sharp scissors. When using fur fabric, slide the point of the blade under the pile and cut through the backing and gently separate the pieces to avoid damaging the pile. Fur fabric should always be cut through a single thickness only, but felt or lining can be cut as a double thickness where appropriate. Small openings or holes should be made with embroidery scissors.

MAKING A PATTERN

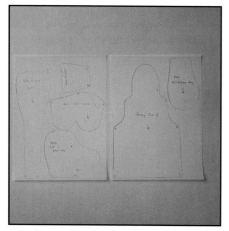

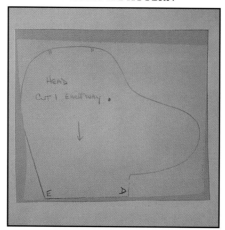

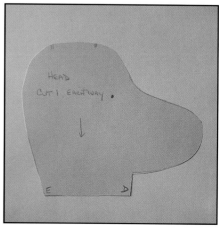

1 Trace the template for the required design from the book onto tracing paper with a pencil, taking care to transfer all markings.

2 Cut a rough square around each shape and then glue the tracing to card.

3 Following the pencil line, cut out card shape. Repeat for each pattern piece. Check all markings have been transferred.

FOLD LINE TRACING

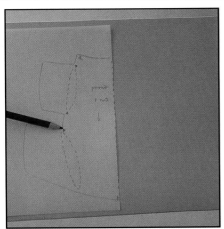

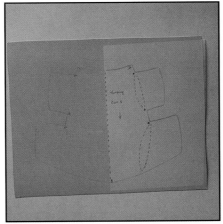

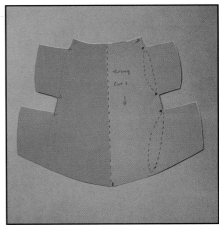

4 *Lay out traced template face down on card (markings towards card) with 'fold line' to centre. Draw around shape, omitting 'fold line.'*

5 *Carefully turn the pattern over, keeping fold line to centre. Glue into position.*

6 *Cut the pattern out as one piece (see KERRY the KOALA on p.48).*

JOINING TEMPLATE PIECES

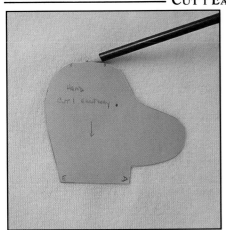

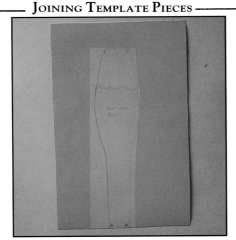

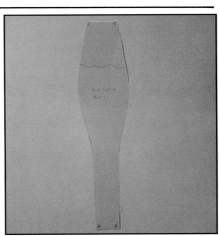

7 *Trace around separate templates on to tracing paper as shown. Cut out and trim along wavy lines (see Jack the Rabbit p.82).*

8 *Matching wavy lines as shown, place both pieces of tracing paper on to a single piece of card. Glue on to card.*

9 *Cut the pattern out as one piece.*

CUT 1 EACH WAY
CUT 2

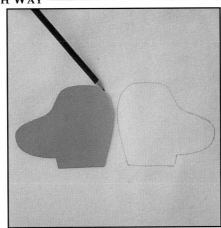

10 *Place the pattern on a single thickness of fabric. Carefully draw around the pattern.*

11 *Turn pattern over as shown and draw around pattern shape again. Cut out the two shapes round the cutting line.*

12 *On a single thickness of fabric, lay out pattern and draw around it. Lift pattern, keeping the same side facing, and lay on fabric. Draw around again. Cut out.*

Sewing Techniques

SEAM ALLOWANCE
A seam allowance of 6mm (¼″) is included on the pattern pieces.

STITCHING LINE
The stitching line is 6mm (¼″) in from the edge of the fabric unless otherwise indicated.

SEAMS
Seams may be sewn by hand or by machine. All the seams on the puppets in this book have been sewn on an ordinary domestic sewing machine and finished by hand oversewing or a zigzag machine stitch. Full sewing instructions are given in the step-by-step guide for each puppet.

Throughout the book in the step-by-step instructions seams have been pinned, using extra-long glass-headed pins, and sewn straight from pinning. Beginners could tack the seams before sewing, removing the tacking threads after stitching. For photographic purposes seams have not been finished off but **to ensure that seams do not open, machine stitching should be reversed for approximately 6mm (¼″) at each end.**

Begin sewing a seam by pinning together the two pieces to be joined, right sides facing together. As each section of seam is sewn, remove pins as appropriate. Fur seams should be brushed out with a teazle brush.

NOTE: *For photographic purposes a contrasting thread has been used to show the stitching line. However, a matching or toning thread should always be used for sewing the puppets.*

EASE POINT
Curved or angled seams may need to be snipped to the stitching line with scissors in order to ease the fabric. Care should be taken not to snip the stitching line (see step 16 p.38).

STITCHES
○ **Backstitch** should be used when sewing seams by hand as this produces a strong seam which will not break.

○ **Oversewing** or **zigzag** stitch should be used to prevent fabric fraying.

○ **Ladder stitch** (see step 3 on p.9) should be used for joining heads to bodies.

THREADS
A matching strong synthetic thread should be used for sewing seams as this will not break when the puppet is turned and filled. The end should be knotted firmly when sewing by hand. Thread can be used double for extra strength. Button thread, or other extra-strong thread, should be used for sewing the head, nose or tail (where appropriate) in place. Stranded embroidery thread is used for embroidering facial features.

FACIAL FEATURES
Careful placement of the facial features will enhance the puppet's appearance and create the appropriate expression and character.

○ **EYES:** Most of the puppets in this book have been fitted with safety eyes (see steps 6-9 p.9). Safety eyes are available in different styles and sizes (see step 4 p.9) and sold complete with plastic or metal washers. When using a knitted fabric, stitch around the hole before the eye is fitted to ensure safety (see step 7 p.9).

○ **NOSES:** Several different styles and sizes of nose are available (see step 5 p.9). Noses can also be made from felt or fabric or embroidered directly on to the fabric (see steps 1-2 p.9).

○ **SQUEAKERS AND RATTLES:** Steps 11-17 on p.14 (*Quackers the duck*) illustrate the fitting of a squeaker. Other instructions are given in the step-by-step guide to each puppet where appropriate.

TURNING AND STUFFING
All seams should be carefully inspected, and the eyes inserted if necessary, before turning right side out. The head should be gently eased through the opening. When turning a full body, the limbs should be turned using the fingers, or a blunt stuffing tool, and then the limbs should be eased through the body opening.

If required, insert the nose before stuffing the puppet. Stuff carefully in accordance with the directions given in the step-by-step instructions. Always stuff slightly harder than required as the stuffing will soften when handled.

LINING
Full instructions are given in the step-by-step guide for lining puppets where appropriate (see steps 42-45 p.41). Soft cotton fabric should be used for lining.

MONKEY MOUTH

1 Bring the needle out at bottom of nose and embroider a line down. Insert needle, come out to the left, then back to bottom. Repeat for the right side.

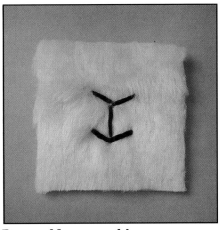

BUNNY NOSE AND MOUTH

2 Work three stitches as for Monkey Mouth, then take needle out at top of straight stitch. Work angled stitches to left and right to match bottom.

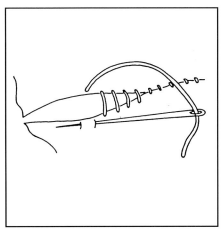

LADDER STITCH

3 Using strong thread, make small stitch 6mm (¼") on side of opening. Make a small stitch on other side. Repeat to end. Pull up tightly and secure.

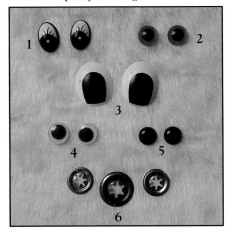

SAFETY EYES

4 1 — Character eyes with lashes. 2 — Teddy eyes. 3 — Large eyes. 4 — Goo goo eyes. 5 — Black rounds. 6 — Assortment of washers.

NOSES

5 1 — Heart. 2 — Cat noses. 3 — Animal nose. 4 — Small round. 5 — Triangular.

FITTING SAFETY EYES AND NOSES

6 Make a very small hole at eye position marked using small pointed scissors.

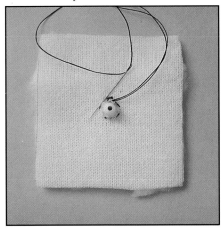

7 Push shank of eye through from right side of material. Turn to right side and check position on the face. On stretchy material, stitch around opening.

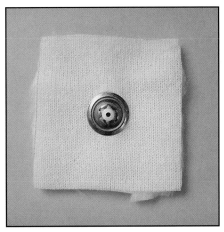

8 Position washer over shank. Lock washer against back of eye pressing down hard, keeping the washer level, to engage the teeth against shank.

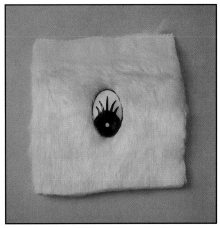

9 With right side facing, gently ease out any fur which has become trapped around the eye.

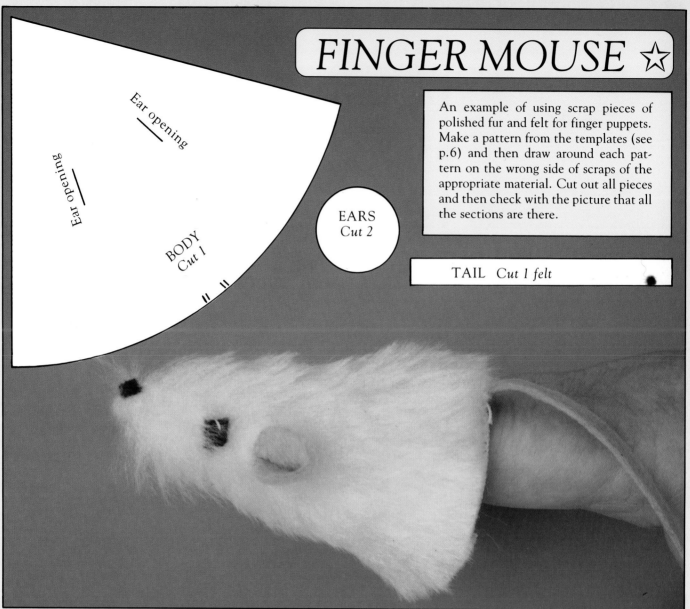

FINGER MOUSE ☆

Ear opening

Ear opening

BODY
Cut 1

EARS
Cut 2

An example of using scrap pieces of polished fur and felt for finger puppets. Make a pattern from the templates (see p.6) and then draw around each pattern on the wrong side of scraps of the appropriate material. Cut out all pieces and then check with the picture that all the sections are there.

TAIL *Cut 1 felt*

1 Fold ears in half and pin. Cut ear openings and insert folded ear into each side. Pin and stitch in position.

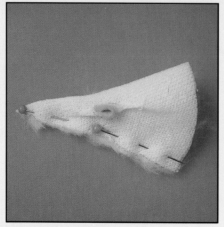

2 Fold in half, right sides facing, and pin along straight edge. Stitch together.

3 Turn right side out and brush seam. Stitch on tail and then small circles of felt for the eyes and nose.

QUACKERS *the* DUCK☆☆

MATERIALS
○ Yellow Polished Fur 385mm (15″) × 385mm (15″).
○ Yellow Felt 75mm (3″) × 75mm (3″).
○ White Lining 110mm (4½″) × 90mm (3½″).
○ 2 Small Goo Goo Eyes.
○ 1 Squeaker.

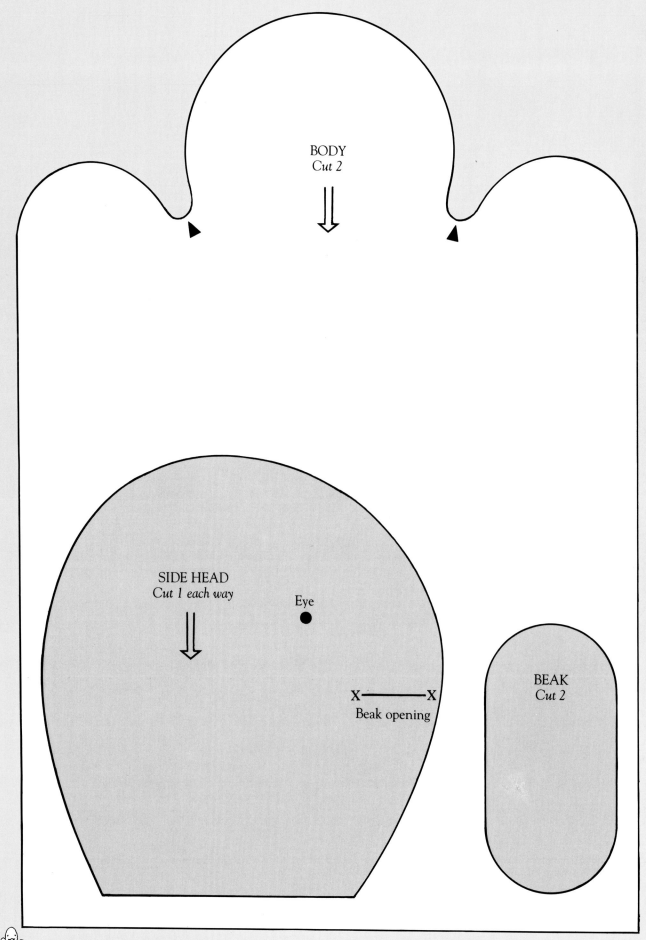

BODY
Cut 2

SIDE HEAD
Cut 1 each way

Eye

X———X
Beak opening

BEAK
Cut 2

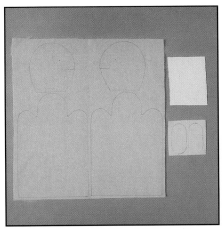

1 Make a pattern of each template shape required (see p.6). Then draw around each pattern on the wrong side of the appropriate material, as shown.

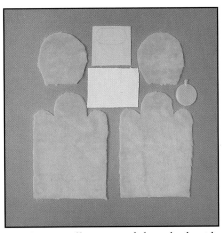

2 Cut out all pieces and then check with the picture that all the sections are there.

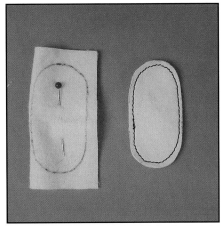

3 Fold over and pin the felt beak. Stitch just inside the marked line, then cut along the line as shown.

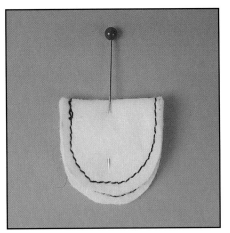

4 Fold the beak in half then position the lower beak slightly forward and pin.

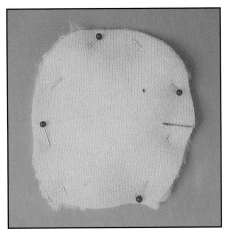

5 Pin each side head piece together around top and sides, right sides facing.

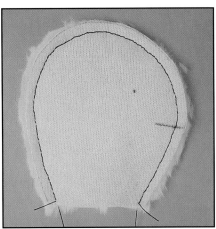

6 Stitch the two pieces together leaving the neck open.

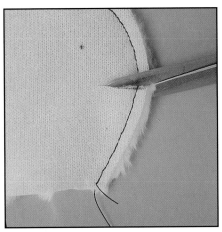

7 Cut along the beak opening, from **X** to **X**, with a pair of sharp scissors.

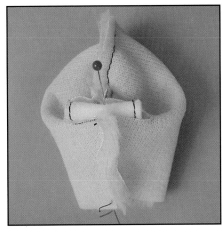

8 With the short beak uppermost, insert beak into the opening until the fold is just visible. Pin to secure.

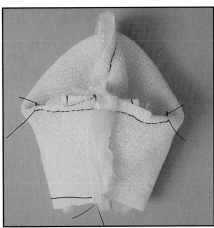

9 Carefully stitch the beak in position tapering off ends. Insert eyes (see p.8).

10 Turn the head right side out. Brush all seams.

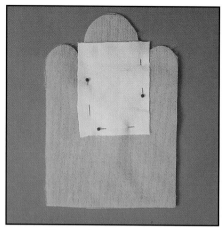

11 Place and pin the white material to the wrong side of a body piece, leave top open.

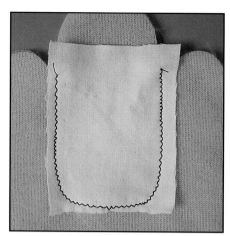

12 Stitch the material, using a zigzag stitch, leaving top open to make a pocket.

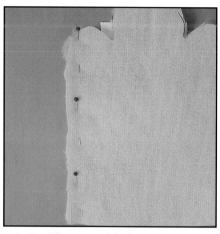

13 Place second body on top, right sides facing, and pin down left side as shown.

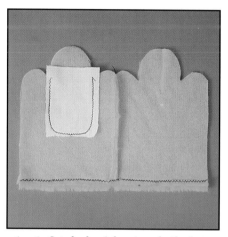

14 Stitch along the pinned side then unfold. Turn up the bottom edge and stitch into place with zigzag stitch.

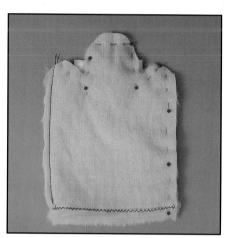

15 Fold in half and pin along top and right side as shown.

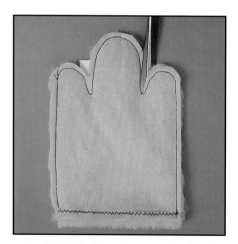

16 Stitch along the top and right side, leaving the bottom open. Carefully cut the two ease points.

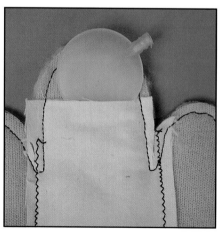

17 Slide the squeaker into the pocket until it reaches the bottom.

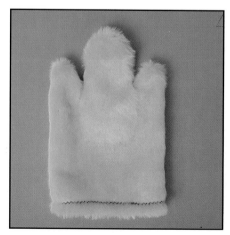

18 Turn the body right side out and brush all seams.

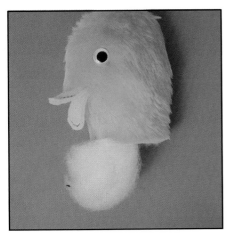

19 Insert a small amount of filling into the front side of the head.

20 Place hand into body then push the neck into the head.
Ensure the squeaker is in the front.

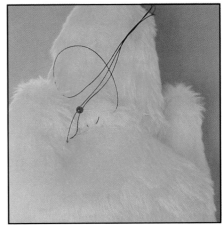

21 Keeping neck well into the head stitch together along the neck edge with ladder stitch as shown. Brush all seams.

MUMMY and DADDY MOUSE ☆☆☆

MATERIALS

DADDY MOUSE

○ Grey Polished Fur 275mm (11″) × 250mm (10″).

○ White Polished Fur 180mm (7″) × 75mm (3″).

○ Pink Felt for Nightcap 250mm (10″) × 180mm (7″).

○ Striped Material 385mm (15″) × 300mm (12″).

○ White Lining 385mm (15″) × 300mm (12″).

○ Small piece Black Felt.

○ Small piece Yellow Felt.

○ 1 White Bobble.

○ 2 Small Black Eyes.

○ ½ metre Ribbon.

MATERIALS

MUMMY MOUSE

○ Grey Polished Fur 275mm (11″) × 250mm (10″).

○ Pink Polished Fur 180mm (7″) × 75mm (3″).

○ Patterned Material 385mm (15″) × 275mm (11″).

○ White Lining 385mm (15″) × 275mm (11″).

○ Thin Cotton for Bonnet 300mm (12″) × 100mm (4″).

○ Lace 1 metre × 12mm (½″).

○ Pink Felt 125mm (5″) × 75mm (3″).

○ 2 Small Black Eyes.

○ 1 White Bobble.

○ ½ metre Ribbon.

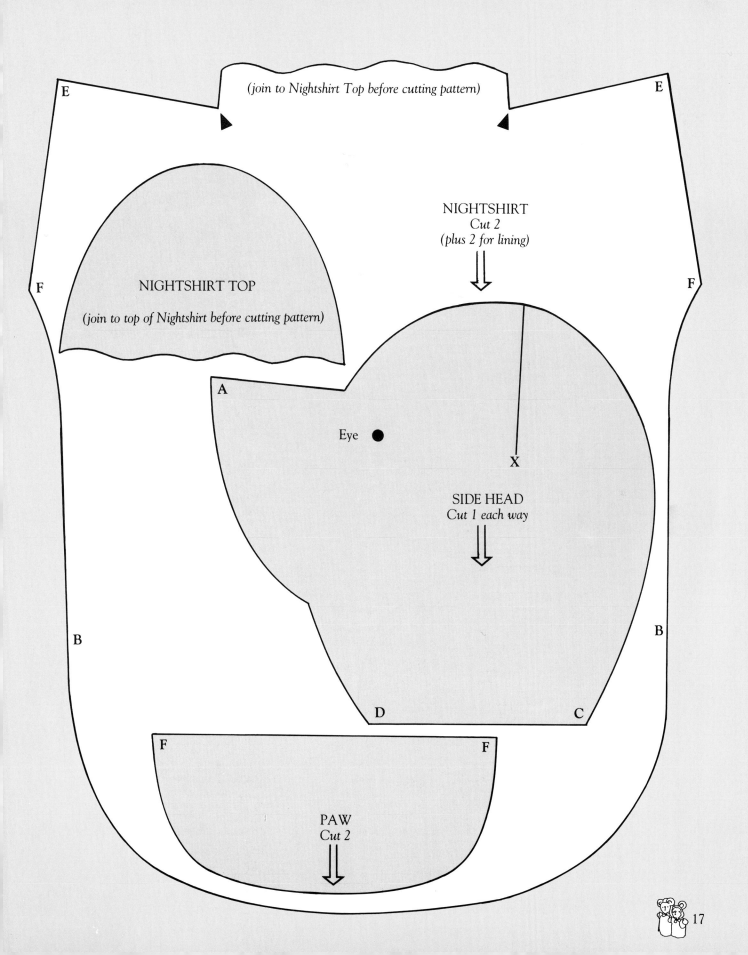

E

(join to Nightshirt Top before cutting pattern)

E

NIGHTSHIRT
Cut 2
(plus 2 for lining)

F

NIGHTSHIRT TOP

(join to top of Nightshirt before cutting pattern)

F

A

Eye ●

X

SIDE HEAD
Cut 1 each way

B

B

D

C

F

F

PAW
Cut 2

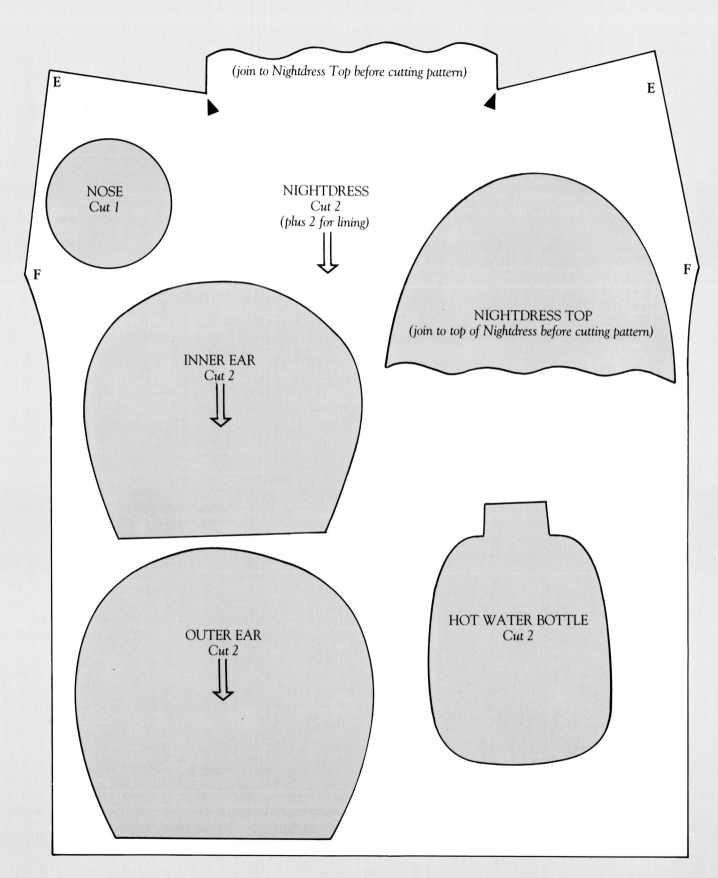

E

(join to Nightdress Top before cutting pattern)

E

NOSE
Cut 1

NIGHTDRESS
Cut 2
(plus 2 for lining)

F

NIGHTDRESS TOP
(join to top of Nightdress before cutting pattern)

F

INNER EAR
Cut 2

OUTER EAR
Cut 2

HOT WATER BOTTLE
Cut 2

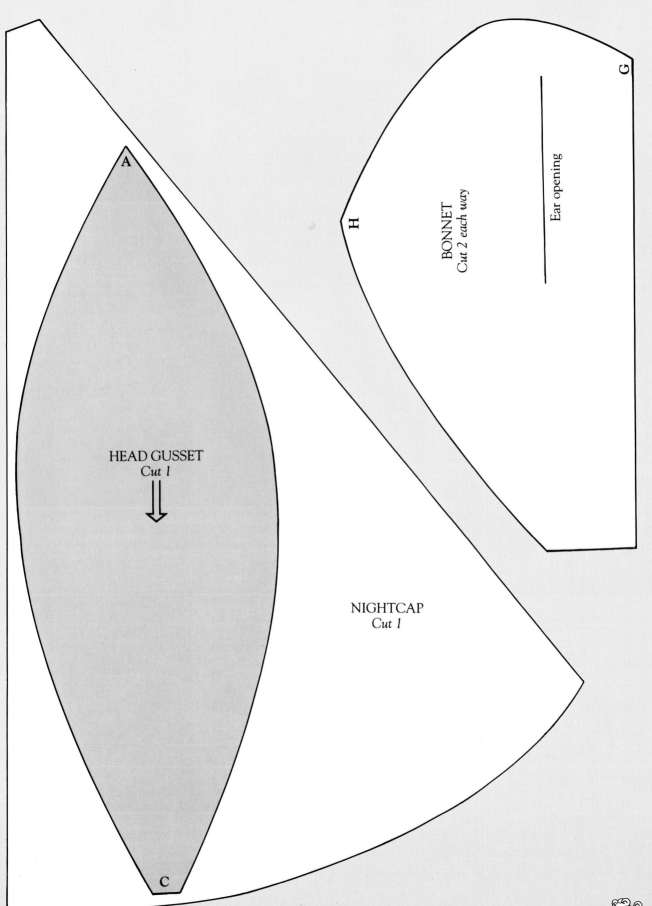

A

HEAD GUSSET
Cut 1

⇓

C

G

BONNET
Cut 2 each way

Ear opening

H

NIGHTCAP
Cut 1

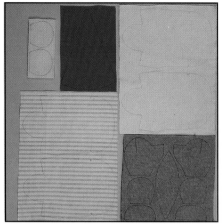

1 Make a pattern of each template shape required (see p. 6) for Daddy Mouse. Then draw around each pattern on the wrong side of the appropriate material, as shown.

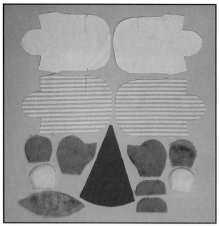

2 Cut out all pieces and then check with the picture that all the sections are there.

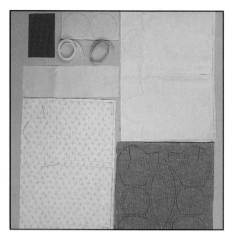

3 Make a pattern of each template shape required (see p. 6) for Mummy Mouse. Then draw around each pattern on the wrong side of the appropriate material, as shown.

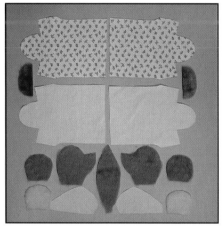

4 Cut out all pieces and then check with the picture that all the sections are there.

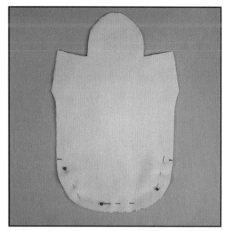

5 Pin a nightshirt lining to a nightshirt fabric, right sides facing. Pin from B to B, along the bottom edge.

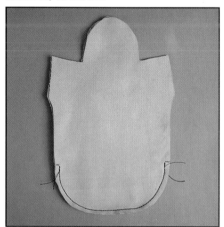

6 Stitch along the bottom edge of the nightshirt as shown.

7 Carefully snip at B to seam line on each side of the nightshirt. Repeat steps 4-7 for second side. Turn each piece right side out.

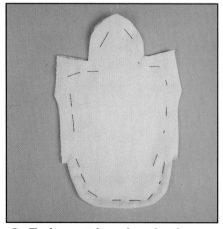

8 Tack material matching the edges. Repeat steps 5-8 for second side.

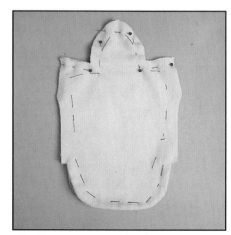

9 Pin top edge together from E to E, right sides facing.

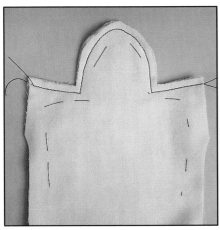

10 Stitch along the top edge from **E** to **E** joining the two sides together.

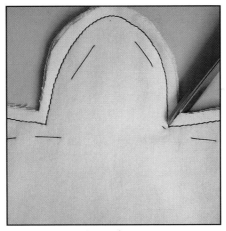

11 Snip at the neck corners to ease the seams. Unfold the nightshirt to the right side and lay flat.

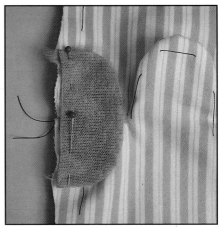

12 Pin a paw to each side matching mark **F** to **F**, right sides facing.

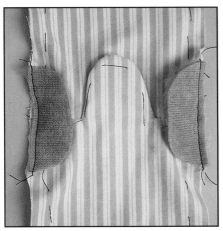

13 Stitch each paw to nightshirt, tapering off each side as shown.

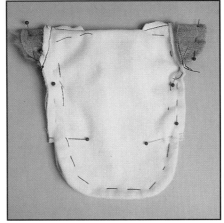

14 Open out the paws, then fold nightshirt in half, right sides facing. Pin each side together from centre paw to position mark **B**.

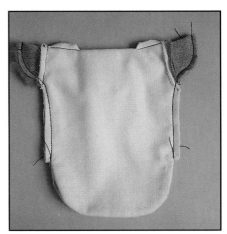

15 Stitch from top to **B**, on each side of the nightshirt. Carefully remove the tacking stitches.

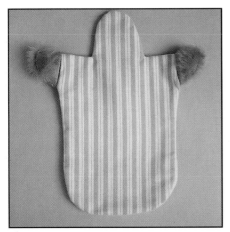

16 Turn right side out and check that all seams are correctly stitched. Brush the fur paws then press nightshirt with a cool iron.

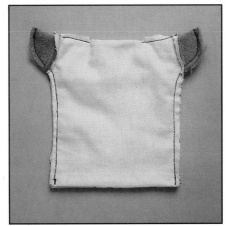

17 Repeat steps 5-15 for the nightdress of Mummy Mouse.

18 Turn right side out. Press material. Stitch lace along bottom edge. Brush the fur paws.

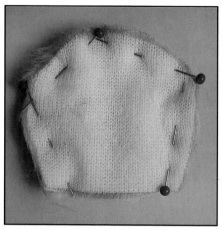

19 *Using Daddy Mouse materials, pin each inner ear to each outer ear right sides facing, as shown.*

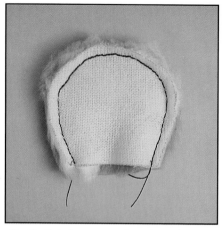

20 *Stitch ears together along the outer edge, leaving bottom open.*

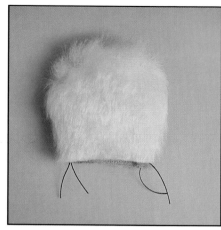

21 *Turn each ear right side out and brush all seams.*

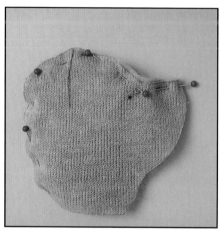

22 *Starting at mark* **A** *pin side head to head gusset finishing at mark* **C**.

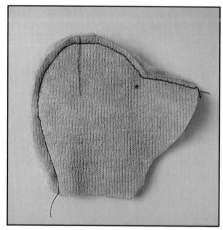

23 *Carefully stitch side head to head gusset as shown. Turn head over with gusset uppermost.*

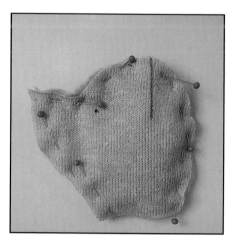

24 *Pin second side head to gusset, from mark* **D** *to mark* **C**.

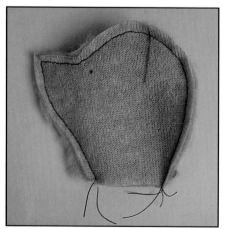

25 *Carefully stitch the pieces together leaving the bottom open, as shown.*

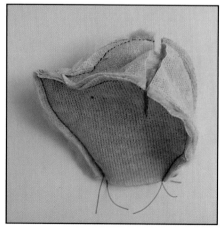

26 *Starting at* **X** *on side head, carefully cut ear opening across top of head gusset and down to* **X** *on second side.*

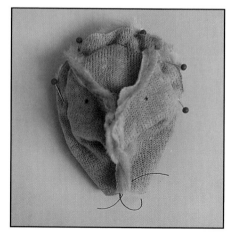

27 *Insert ears (with inner ears facing towards nose), into ear opening and pin into position. Then pin seam from* **X** *to* **X**.

28 Stitch ear opening seams, tapering off as shown.

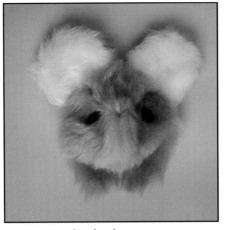

29 Turn head right out, insert eyes (see p.8), then brush all seams.

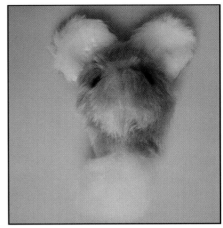

30 Stuff the front half of the head to fill-out the face.

31 Insert hand into nightshirt and place head over the top piece, keeping the stuffing forward.

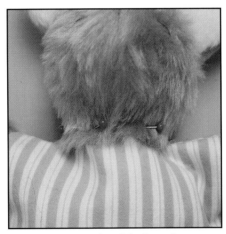

32 Align head with body and pin in position around the neck, using seam allowance as shown.

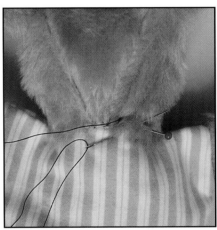

33 Keeping hand in puppet, stitch carefully and firmly around the neck with ladder stitch. Secure thread.

34 With strong thread, sew running stitch around edge of felt for nose.

35 Place small amount of stuffing in centre, pull up thread and fasten. Roll between hands to make round nose shape.

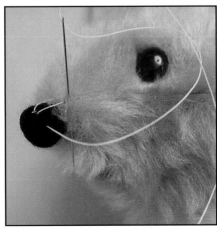

36 Stitch nose firmly into place with ladder stitch as shown.

37 *Picture shows Daddy Mouse so far.*

38 *Repeat steps 19-36 using the materials for Mummy Mouse.*

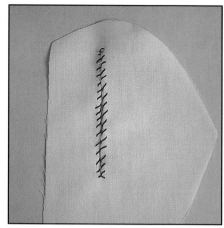

39 *Cut ear opening in bonnet. Over-sew the cut edges to neaten, as shown. Repeat for second side.*

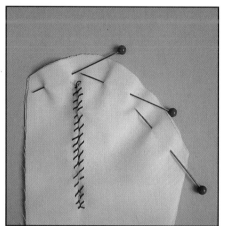

40 *Place both sides together and pin from **H** to **G**.*

41 *Stitch from **G** to **H**, open out. Then stitch lace around outer edge.*

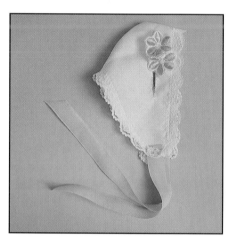

42 *Stitch ribbon to short side and flowers near top of ear opening, as shown. Tie onto Mummy Mouse's head.*

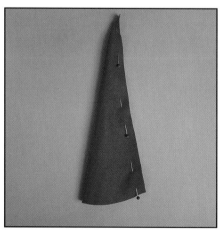

43 *Fold nightcap in half and pin along edge.*

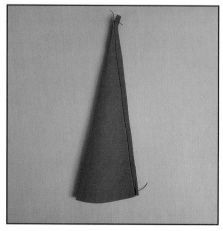

44 *Stitch the long edge together to form the nightcap shape.*

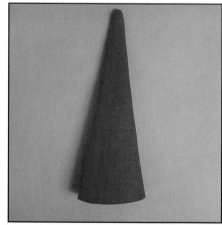

45 *Turn right side out and pull into shape.*

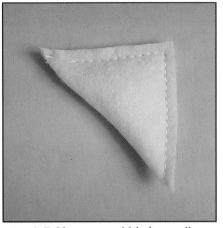

46 Stitch a bobble to top. Lightly stuff and then sew onto Daddy Mouse's head. Tie ribbon around neck.

47 Fold a square of felt diagonally, insert small amount of stuffing and stitch along edges to make a cheese, as shown. Sew to Daddy Mouse's paw.

48 Pin hot water bottle sides together with small amount of filling in centre. Stitch around edge and then sew it to Mummy Mouse's paw.

CLEO the CAT ☆☆☆

MATERIALS

○ Leopard Fur 475mm (19″) × 405mm (16″).

○ 2 Small Black Eyes.

○ 1 Cat Nose.

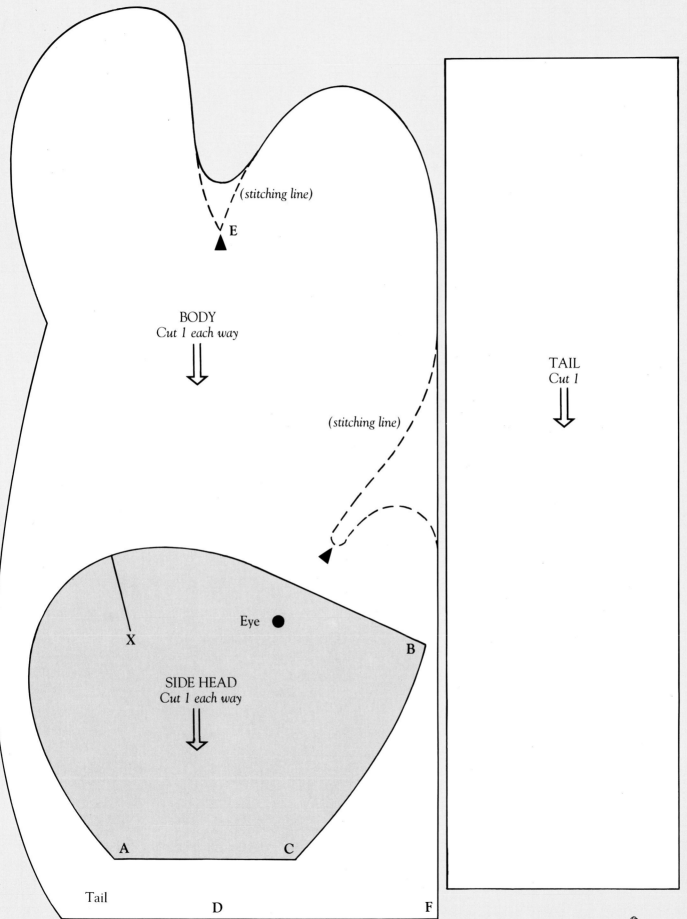

(stitching line)

▲ E

BODY
Cut 1 each way
⇓

(stitching line)

TAIL
Cut 1
⇓

Eye ●

X

B

SIDE HEAD
Cut 1 each way
⇓

A   C

Tail

D   F

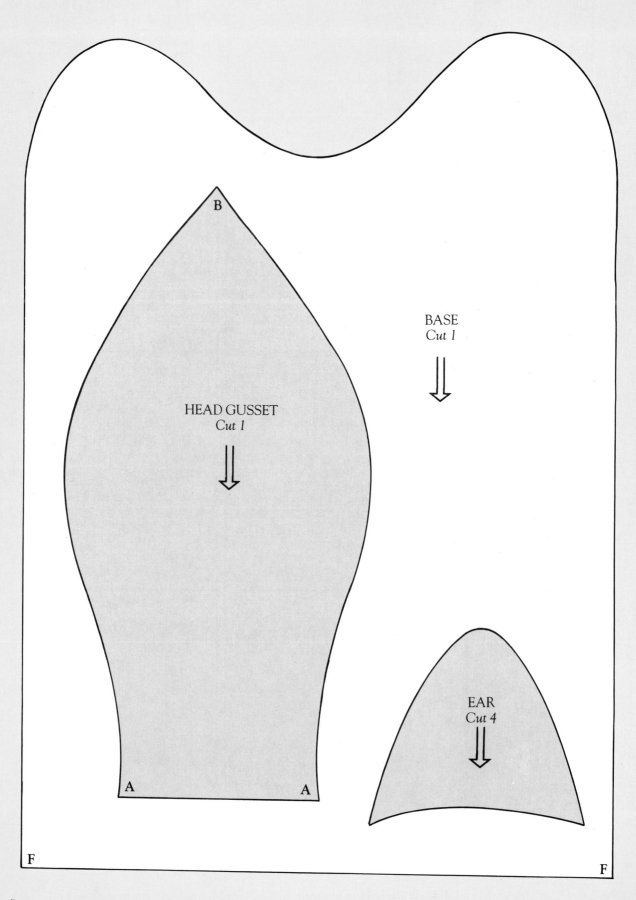

BASE
Cut 1
⇓

HEAD GUSSET
Cut 1
⇓

B

A   A

EAR
Cut 4
⇓

F   F

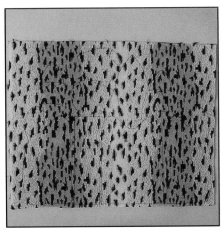

1 Make a pattern of each template shape required (see p.6). Then draw around each pattern on the wrong side of the material, as shown.

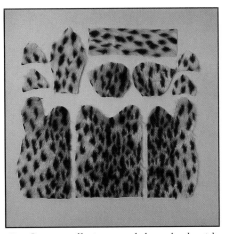

2 Cut out all pieces and then check with the picture that all the sections are there.

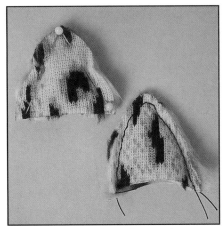

3 Pin, then stitch, each pair of ears together, right sides facing, leaving bottom open.

4 Turn each ear right side out and brush all seams.

5 Pin head gusset to side head starting at mark **B** and finishing at **A**.

6 Carefully stitch the head gusset to the side head. Then open out the head gusset.

7 Pin and stitch the second side head to the head gusset from mark **A** to **C**. Leave the bottom open.

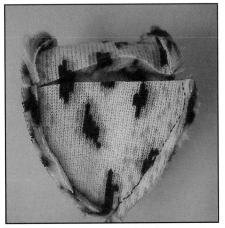

8 Starting at **X** on side head, carefully cut ear opening across top of head gusset and down to **X** on second side head.

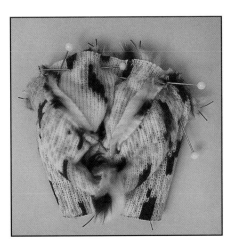

9 Insert ears into ear opening and pin into place. Pin seam from **X** to **X**.

10 Stitch ear opening seam tapering off ends. Insert eyes (see p. 8).

11 Gently turn head right side out and insert nose. Brush all seams.

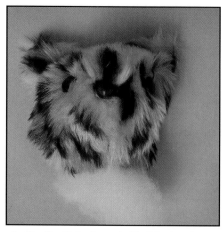

12 Stuff the front half of the head firmly to fill-out the face. Keep back of head free for fingers.

13 Fold and pin tail in half lengthways, right sides together, leaving one end open.

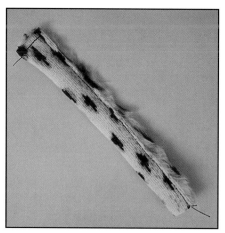

14 Stitch along the pin line and one end.

15 Carefully turn tail right side out, using the blunt end of a knitting needle. Brush the seam.

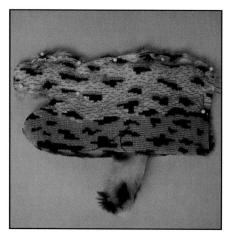

16 Pin the tail in position on side body. Pin second side body to first, from mark **D** to **E**, right sides facing.

17 Stitch from **D**, over body and along stitch line, to **E**. Then snip to seam allowance at **E**.

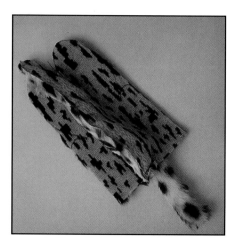

18 Open out the body and place onto the base, right sides facing.

19 Pin down the left side of the body from top of paw to mark **F**.

20 Stitch together, following the seam line from **F** to paw.

21 Open out the body, turn up the bottom edge and sew into place with zigzag stitch.

22 Refold body and pin from paw then under the neck to **F**, following the stitching line.

23 Carefully stitch, leaving the bottom edge open.

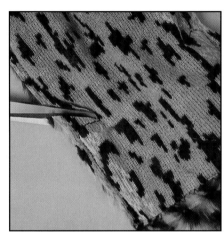

24 With sharp scissors, cut to stitching line at ease points on each side of the body.

25 Then cut to stitching line at ease points under the neck.

26 Push neck and limbs into the centre of the body.

27 Turn right side out and brush all seams.

28 Place hand inside body and then position head over neck, keeping the filling to the front.

29 Turn up seam allowance on head and carefully pin to the neck.

30 Stitch the head to the body, using a ladder stitch and secure thread. Brush all over.

EMMA the ELEPHANT ☆☆☆☆

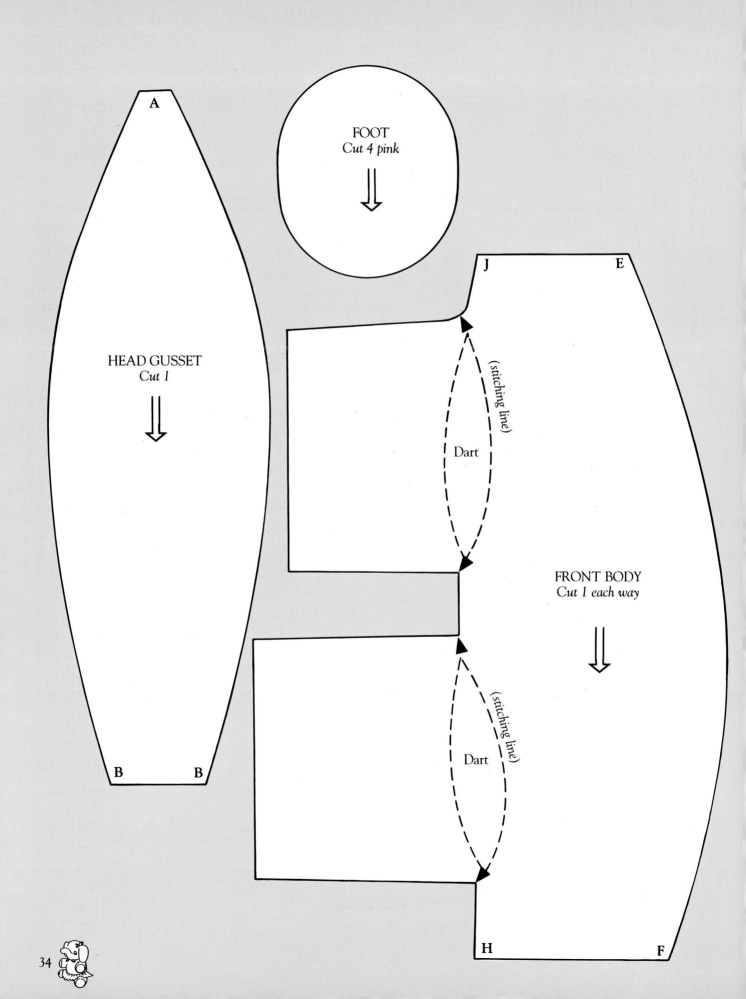

A

FOOT
Cut 4 pink

HEAD GUSSET
Cut 1

B   B

J   E

(stitching line)

Dart

FRONT BODY
Cut 1 each way

(stitching line)

Dart

H   F

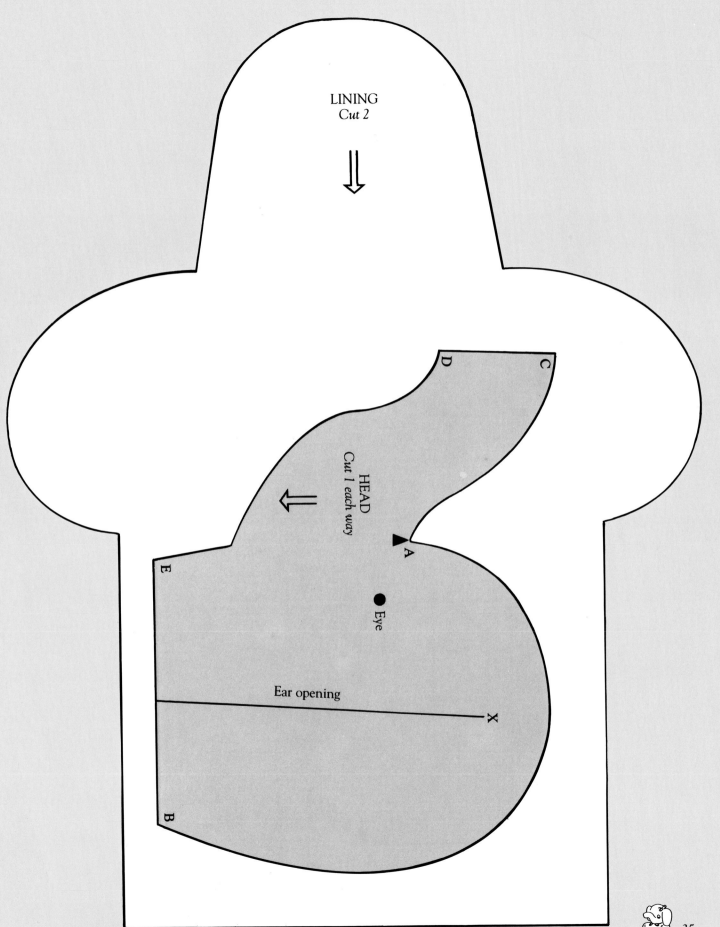

LINING
Cut 2

⇓

D

C

HEAD
Cut 1 each way

⇐

▶ A

● Eye

E

Ear opening

X

B

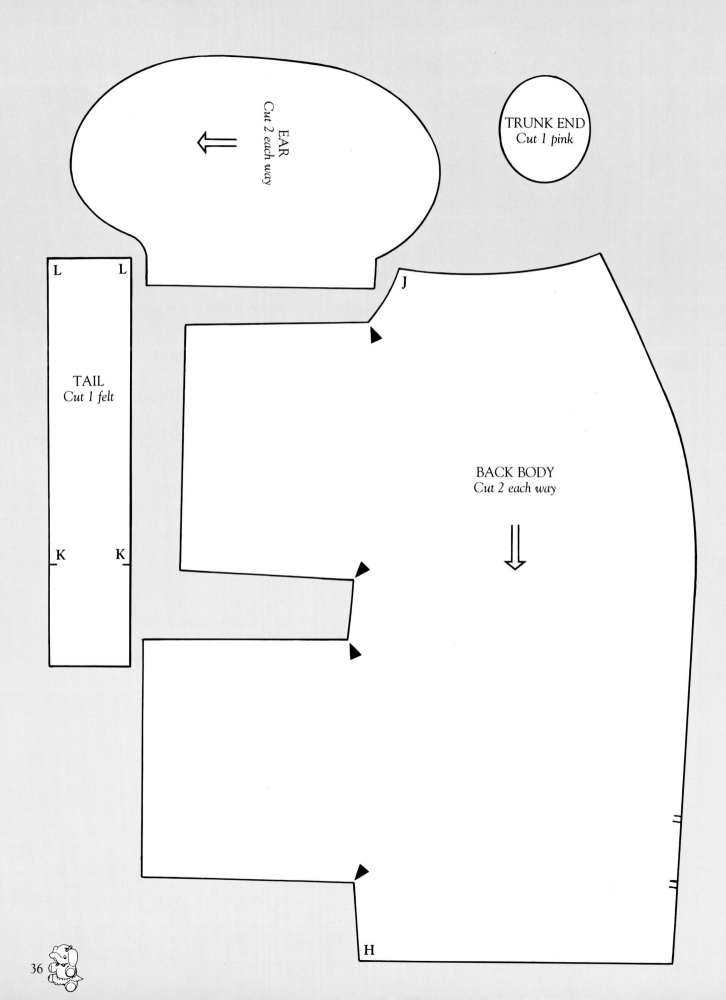

EAR
Cut 2 each way

TRUNK END
Cut 1 pink

L   L

TAIL
Cut 1 felt

K   K

J

BACK BODY
Cut 2 each way

H

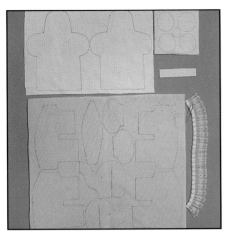

1 Make a pattern of each template shape required (see p.6). Then draw around each pattern on the wrong side of the appropriate material, as shown.

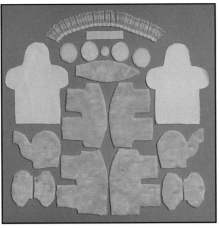

2 Cut out all pieces and then check with the picture that all the sections are there.

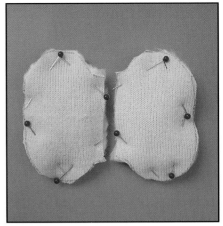

3 Pin ears together right sides facing.

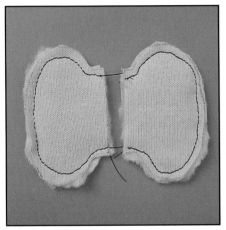

4 Stitch around ears leaving the straight sides open.

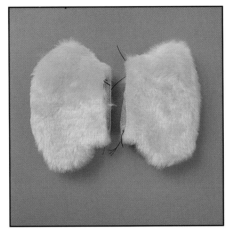

5 Turn the ears right side out, then brush the seams.

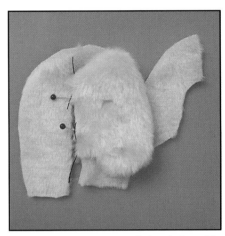

6 Cut ear opening in side head, from X to X. Pin an ear in the position shown.

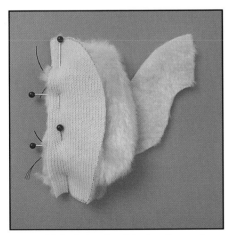

7 Fold the left side of the head over the ear and pin along the opening line.

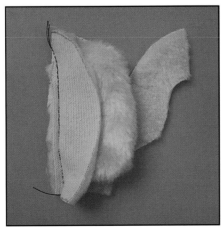

8 Stitch from base to top of head, tapering off to secure the ear in place.

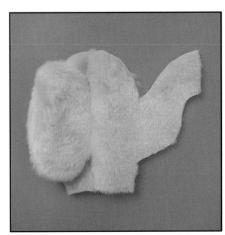

9 Unfold side head and brush the seam. Repeat steps 6-9 for second side head.

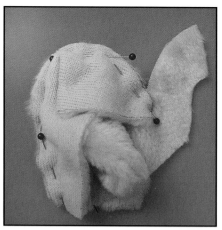

10 Pin head gusset to first side head, right side facing, starting at **B** and continuing to **A**.

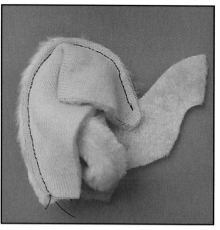

11 Stitch from **B** to **A** to secure the head gusset.

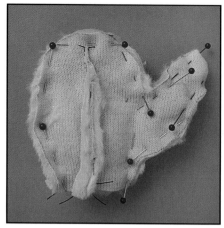

12 Pin second side head to head gusset then trunk to trunk, starting at **B** through to **E**. Leave **C** to **D** open.

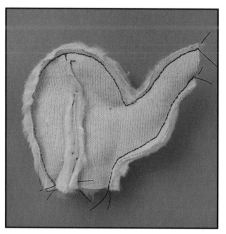

13 Stitch together from **B** to **C**. Then neatly stitch (to keep a good trunk shape) from **D** to **E**.

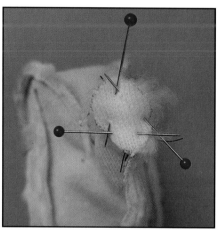

14 Open the tip of the trunk and pin trunk end in position.

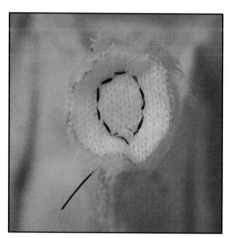

15 Sew together by hand to form a circle of stitches.

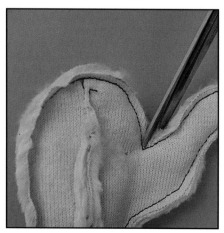

16 Cut to seam line at mark **A**. Insert eyes (see p.8).

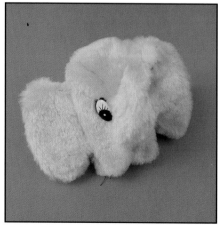

17 Using a blunt pencil, gently push the trunk into the head. Then turn head right side out and brush.

18 Mark front seam (under the trunk) with a single pin, as shown.

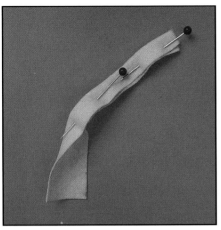

19 Fold tail in half lengthways and pin from **K** to **L**.

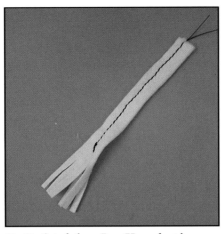

20 Stitch from **L** to **K**, and with sharp scissors fringe wide end of tail.

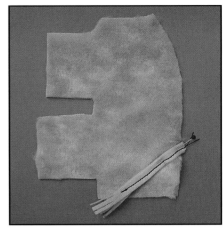

21 Place and pin tail in position on back body, as shown.

22 Place second back body to first, right sides facing, and pin along back seam.

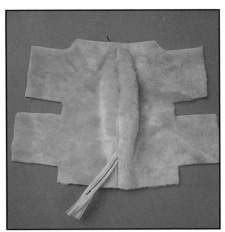

23 Stitch along the back seam. Unfold, check the tail is stitched in position, then brush the seam.

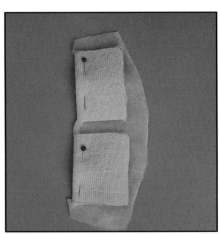

24 On front body fold over the legs to form darts, right sides facing.

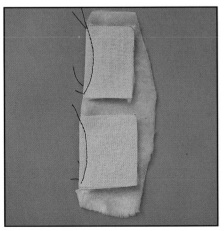

25 Stitch darts following the dotted line and taper off at ends. Repeat steps 24-25 for second front body.

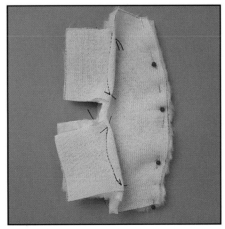

26 Unfold the legs and place the front bodies together, right sides facing. Pin from **E** to **F**.

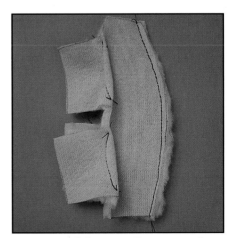

27 Stitch from **F** to **E**, to secure the front seam, as shown. Unfold and brush the seam.

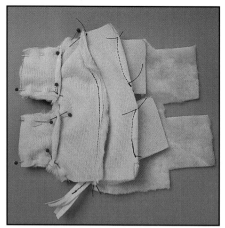

28 Position front body to back body, right sides facing, then pin the left side from **H** to **J**. Leave end of each leg open.

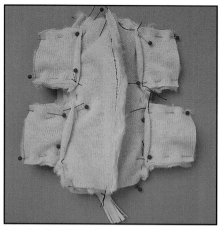

29 Pin the right side together from **J** to **H**, leaving legs, neck and base open.

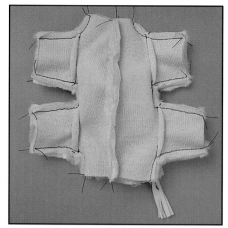

30 Carefully stitch together as shown. Take care not to stitch the tail into the seam.

31 With sharp scissors carefully cut to stitching line at ease points.

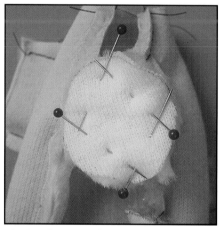

32 Open out the end of one leg and pin a foot to it around the outer edge, right sides facing.

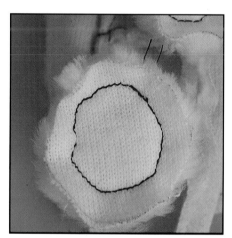

33 Stitch foot neatly to leg. Repeat steps 32-33 for remaining feet.

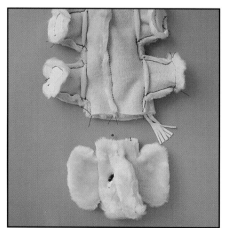

34 Position head below body, as shown.

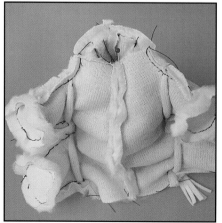

35 Carefully push the head up through the body, until it reaches the neck. Match the pin in the head with mark **E** on body.

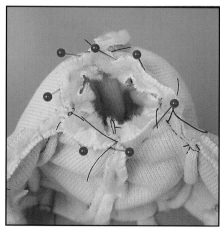

36 Pin around the head, neck and body as shown.

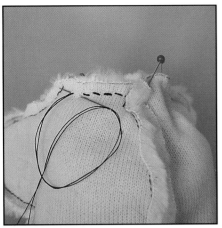

37 Sew by hand the neck to the body, using backstitch.

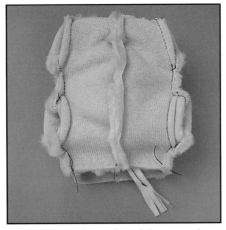

38 Carefully push each leg towards the centre of body, as shown.

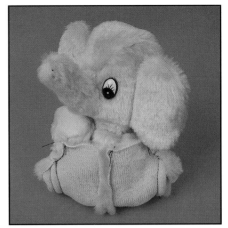

39 Push head down through base to turn the body right side out. Brush all seams.

40 Stuff the trunk firmly with filling. Then stuff the front of the head lightly.

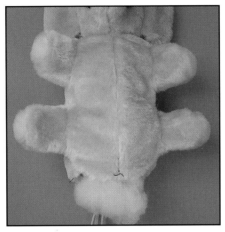

41 Stuff each lower leg firmly and then the tips of each upper leg. Fill tummy well to make a good full shape.

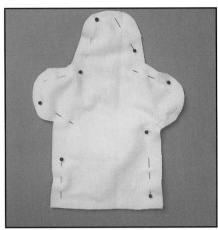

42 Pin both linings together, keeping the base open.

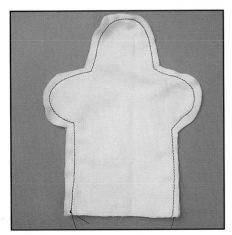

43 Neatly stitch the linings together leaving the base open. Insert a hand between the lining.

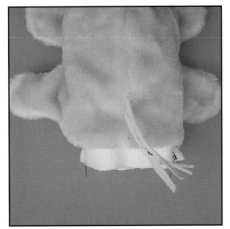

44 With lining on hand insert into the body, ensure the filling is kept to the front of the tummy. Use fingers to ease the lining into position.

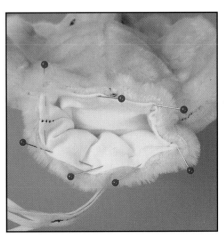

45 Carefully pin the bottom of the lining to the base of the body, using the seam allowance. Stitch together by hand.

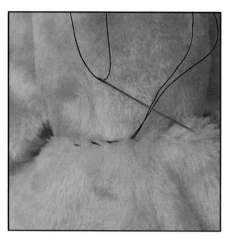

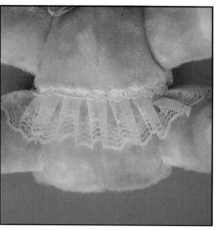

46 *Insert hand into body and sew around neck to secure lining.*

47 *Stitch pleated lace around middle of body to form a tutu.*

48 *Tie ribbon around neck using a double knot and bow. Stitch a flower beside ear, as shown.*

SID the SNAKE ☆

MATERIALS
○ Green Polished Fur 300mm (12″) × 350mm (14″).
○ Green Felt 230mm (9″) × 125mm (5″).
○ Lining 125mm (5″) × 125mm (5″).
○ 1 Rattle.
○ 2 Small Black Eyes.

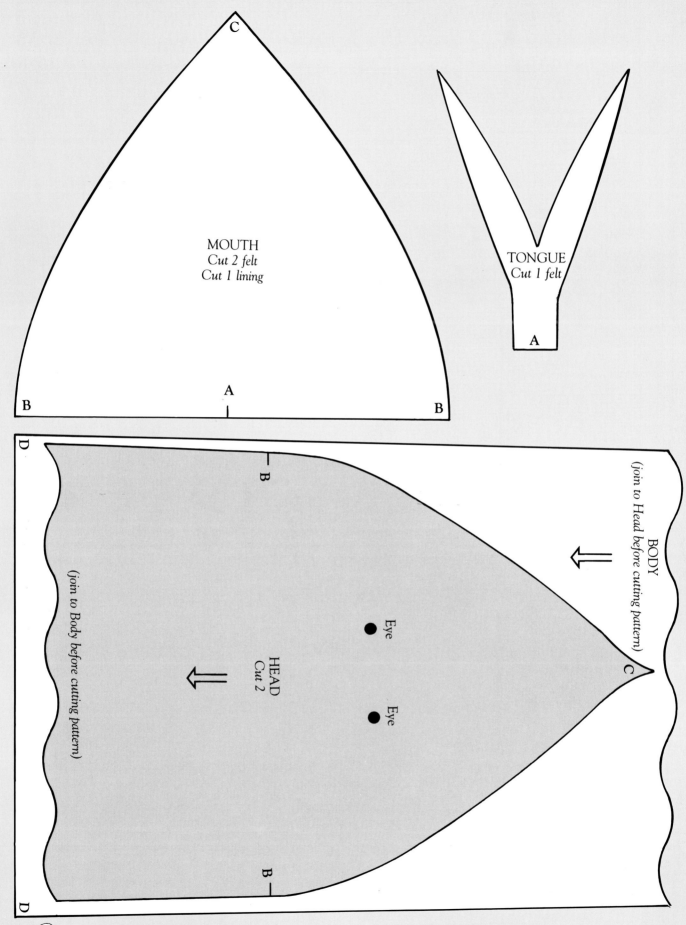

MOUTH
Cut 2 felt
Cut 1 lining

TONGUE
Cut 1 felt

BODY
(join to Head before cutting pattern)

(join to Body before cutting pattern)

Eye

HEAD
Cut 2

Eye

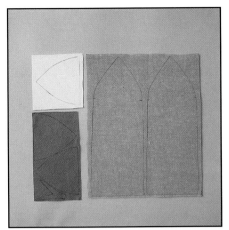

1 Make a pattern of each template shape required (see p.6). Then draw around each pattern on the wrong side of the appropriate material, as shown.

2 Cut out all pieces and then check with the picture that all the sections are there.

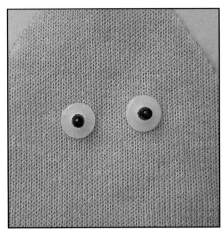

3 Insert eyes (see p.8) in marked position on head.

4 Place the two bodies together, right sides facing. Pin from **D** to **B** and then **B** to **D**.

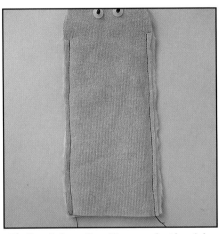

5 Stitch from **B** to **D** on each side of the body, leaving the mouth and base open.

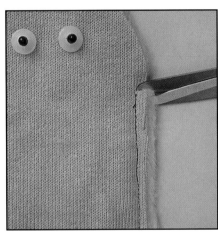

6 Cut to seam line at **B**, on each side of the body.

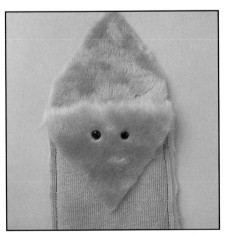

7 Fold back the head (with inserted eyes) to stitch line at **B**.

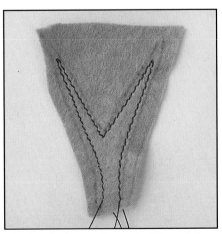

8 Stitch close to the marked line of the tongue.

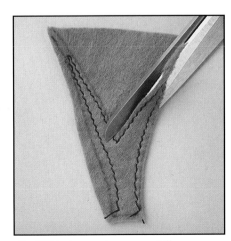

9 With sharp scissors carefully cut out the tongue shape, along the marked line.

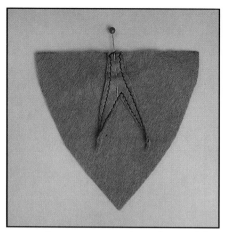

10 Pin tongue in position **A** on a felt mouth.

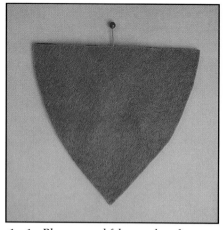

11 Place second felt mouth to first, matching **B** to **B**.

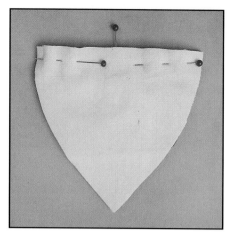

12 Then place the mouth lining on top and pin all pieces together, from **B** to **B**.

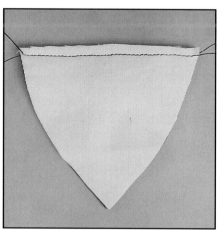

13 Stitch along seam from **B** to **B** taking care to secure the tongue at **A**.

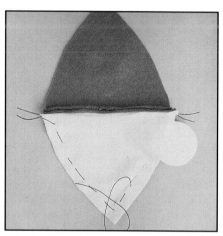

14 Unfold the mouth. Match one felt side with the lining. Tack together along one side, insert rattle then complete the tacking.

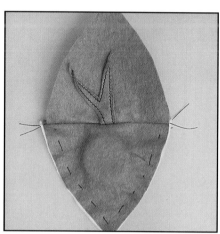

15 Turn mouth over and position rattle centrally, as shown.

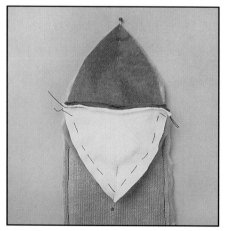

16 Turn mouth over and position onto the head and pin at **C**. The rattle should be on the same side as the inserted eyes.

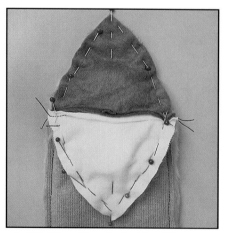

17 Pin at **B** on both sides. Then pin along each side, as shown.

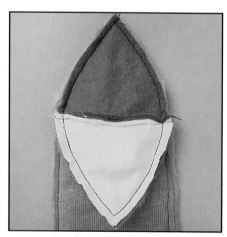

18 Stitch together from **C** to **C** along both sides. Carefully remove the tacking stitches.

19 *Turn right side out by pushing both sides of the mouth into the body.*

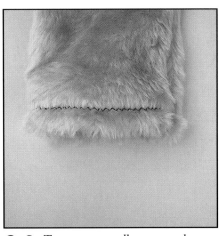

20 *Turn up seam allowance at base and neaten with zigzag stitching.*

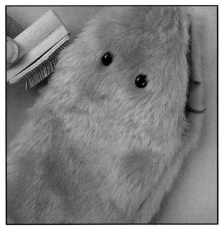

21 *With a teazle brush, brush all seams (do not brush the felt tongue and mouth).*

KERRY the KOALA ☆☆

MATERIALS

○ Polished Long Fur 510mm (20″) × 300mm (12″).

○ Lining 350mm (14″) × 125mm (5″).

○ Black Felt 180mm (7″) × 60mm (2½″).

○ 2 Teddy Eyes.

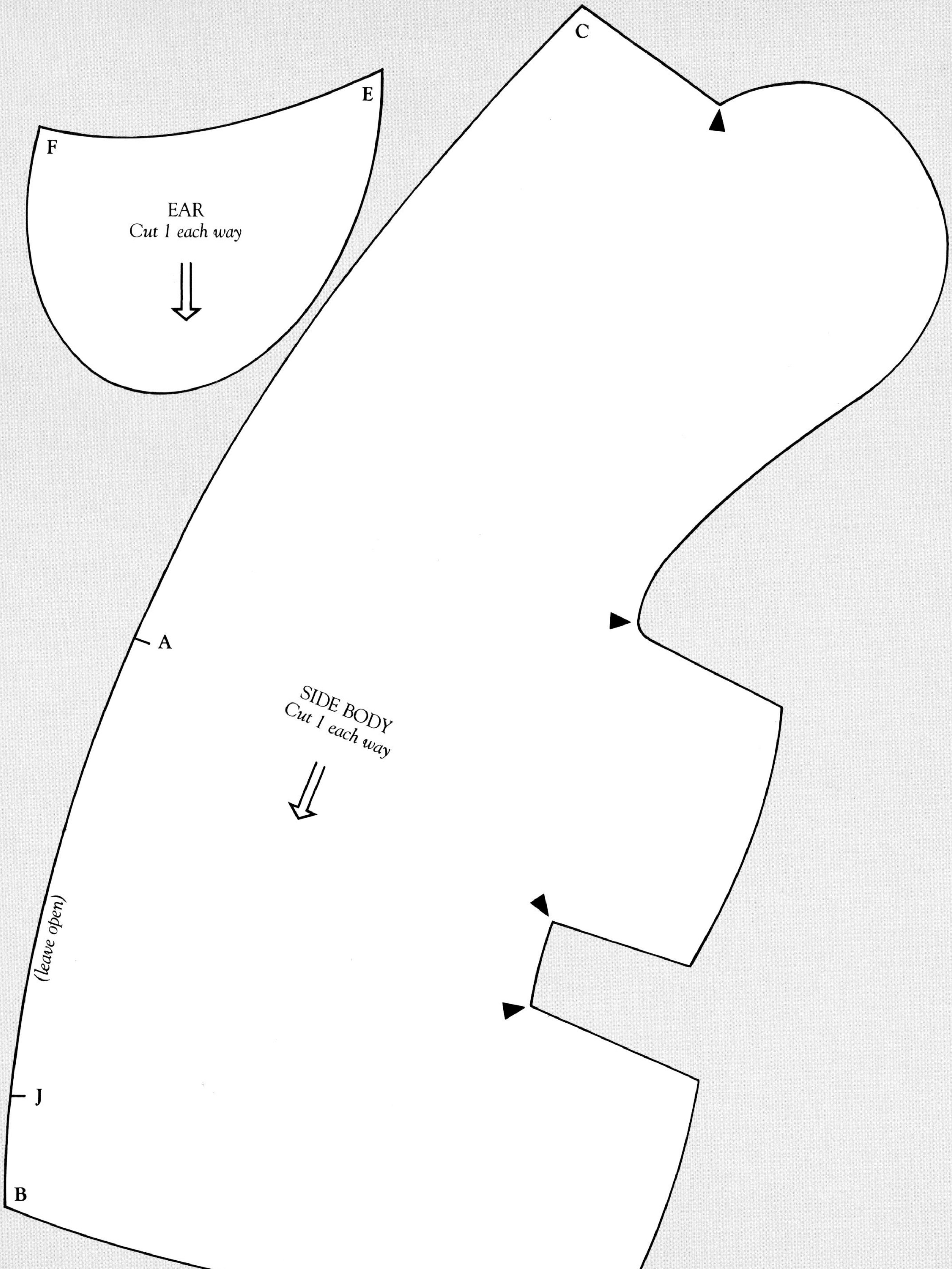

C

E

F

EAR
Cut 1 each way

⇓

A

SIDE BODY
Cut 1 each way

⇓

(leave open)

J

B

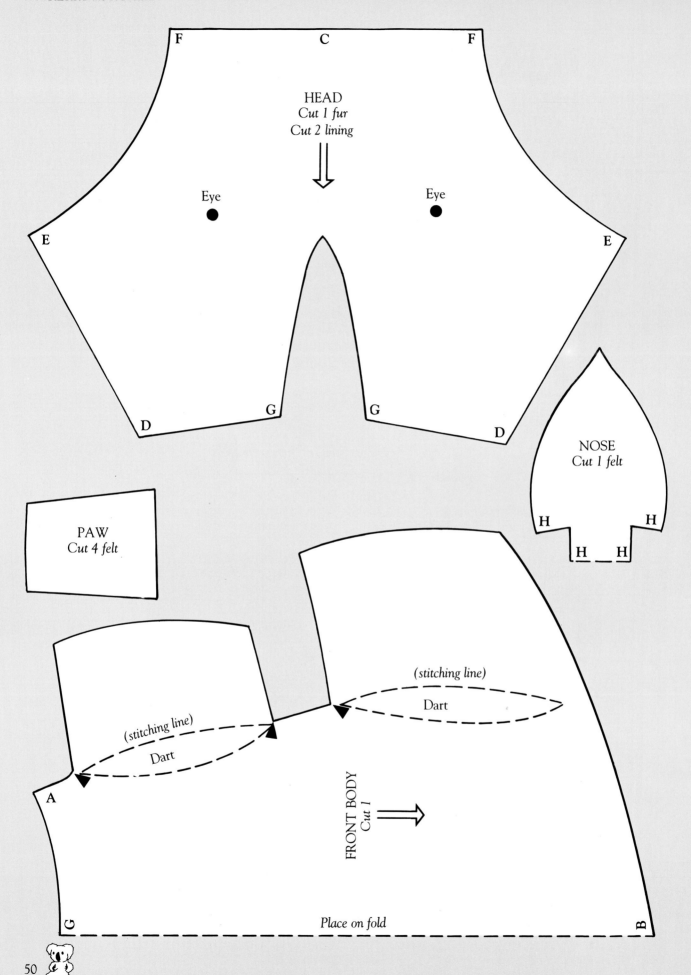

F C F

HEAD
Cut 1 fur
Cut 2 lining

Eye

Eye

E E

G G

D D

NOSE
Cut 1 felt

H H

H H

PAW
Cut 4 felt

(stitching line)

Dart

(stitching line)

Dart

A

FRONT BODY
Cut 1

G

Place on fold

B

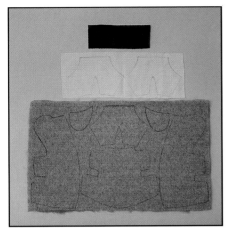

1 Make a pattern of each template shape required (see p. 6). Then draw around each pattern on the wrong side of the appropriate material, as shown.

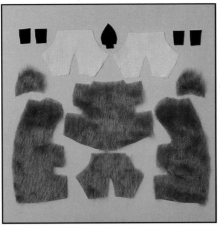

2 Cut out all pieces and check with the picture that all the sections are there.

3 Fold head in half and match **G** to **G**, then pin along seam.

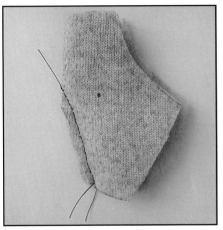

4 Stitch from **G** to top of seam tapering off, as shown. Insert eyes (see p. 8).

5 Fold nose dart from **H** to **H** and pin in place.

6 Stitch the nose dart by hand, then repeat for second side.

7 Unfold to form the domed shape felt nose.

8 Place nose at dart on face. Pin left side of nose to face, then insert a small amount of filling.

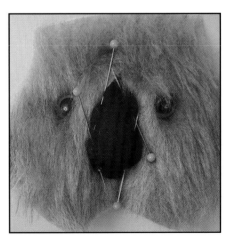

9 Shape filling in nose and pin right side, as shown.

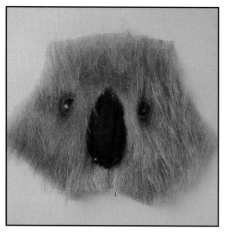

10 *Carefully stitch nose in position by hand, using small stitches. Secure the thread.*

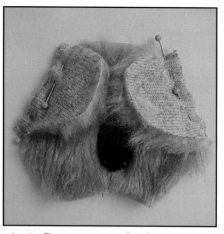

11 *Pin an ear to each side of the face matching **E** to **F**.*

12 *Stitch ears to face. Unfold and brush seams avoiding the felt.*

13 *Fold each limb of the body towards centre, right sides facing, to form darts then pin.*

14 *Stitch each dart tapering off seam line. Unfold and brush all seams.*

15 *Pin face to front of body, right sides facing, matching at **D**, **G** and second **D**. Stitch together.*

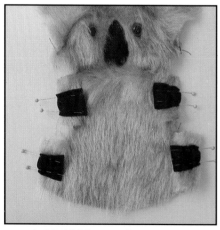

16 *Unfold front and pin short side of each paw to each limb, as shown.*

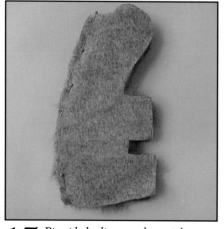

17 *Pin side bodies together, right sides facing, from **B** to **J** and **A** to **C**.*

18 *Stitch together leaving seam open between **J** and **A**.*

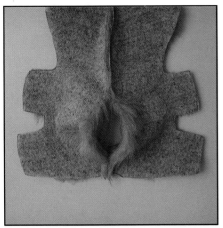

19 Unfold back and, using the seam allowance, neaten the opening by hand sewing. Secure the thread.

20 Place front on back, right sides facing, matching **C** and **B**. Pin along the right side matching **D** at neck. Repeat on left side.

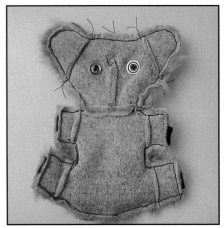

21 Carefully stitch around the edge of the puppet, ensuring the paws are secure in the seam line.

22 Cut to seam line at all the ease points.

23 Turn Kerry right side out by pushing the head through the opening.

24 With sharp scissors cut each felt paw into four pointed claws.

25 Brush all seams carefully avoiding the felt claws.

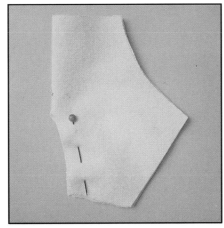

26 Fold each head lining in half then pin and stitch from **G** to top of seam.

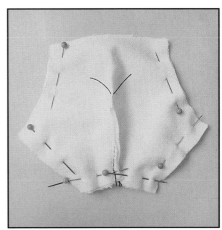

27 Unfold, place and pin each head lining together, right sides facing, from **F** to **D**, **D** to **D** and **D** to **F**, as shown.

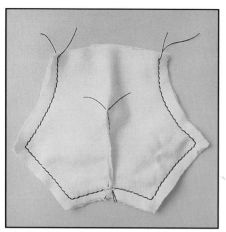

28 Stitch head linings together. Turn right side out.

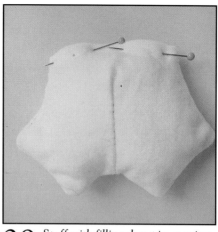

29 Stuff with filling then pin opening together. Stitch and secure.

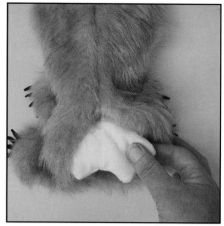

30 Slide the stuffed lining into top of head. Secure in place with a few stitches around the face.

MARVIN *the* MONKEY ☆☆☆☆

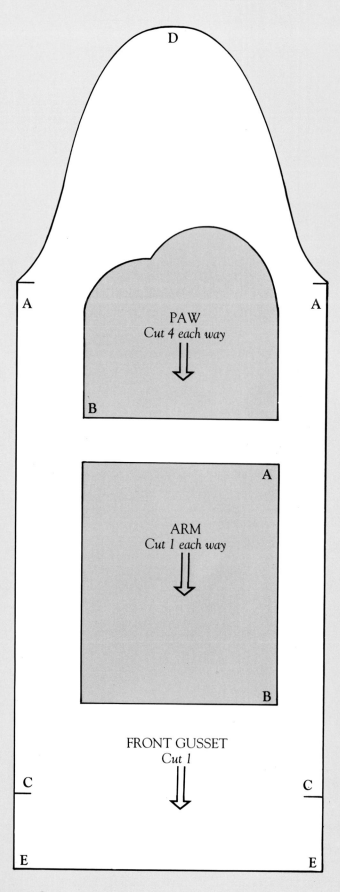

D

A

A

PAW
Cut 4 each way

⇓

B

A

ARM
Cut 1 each way

⇓

B

FRONT GUSSET
Cut 1

⇓

C

C

E

E

L

L

HEAD GUSSET
Cut 1

⇓

K

K

TAIL
Cut 1

⇓

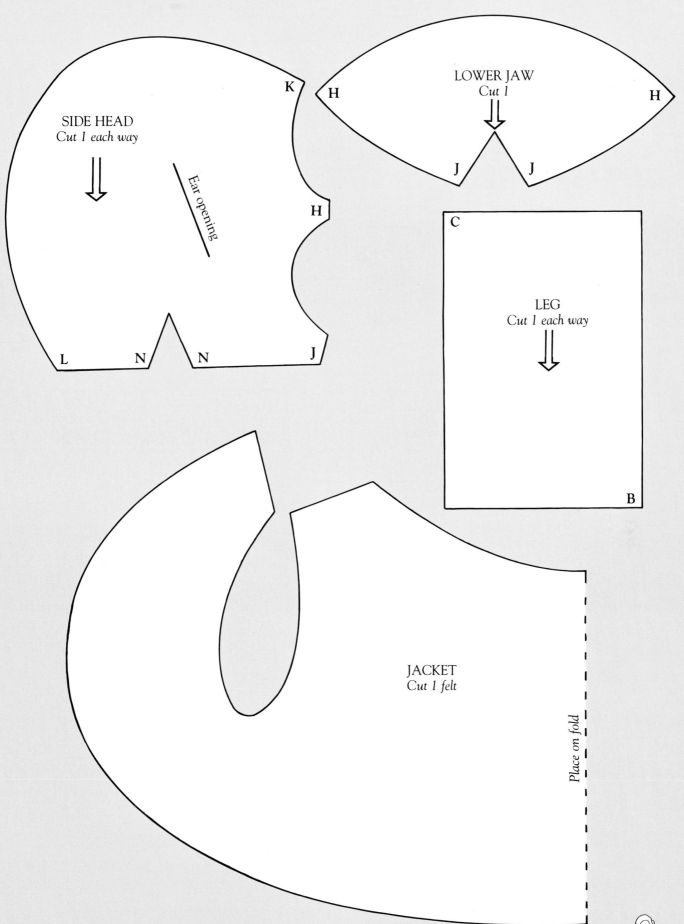

SIDE HEAD
Cut 1 each way

K

H

Ear opening

H

L   N   N   J

LOWER JAW
Cut 1

H

H

J   J

C

LEG
Cut 1 each way

B

JACKET
Cut 1 felt

Place on fold

57

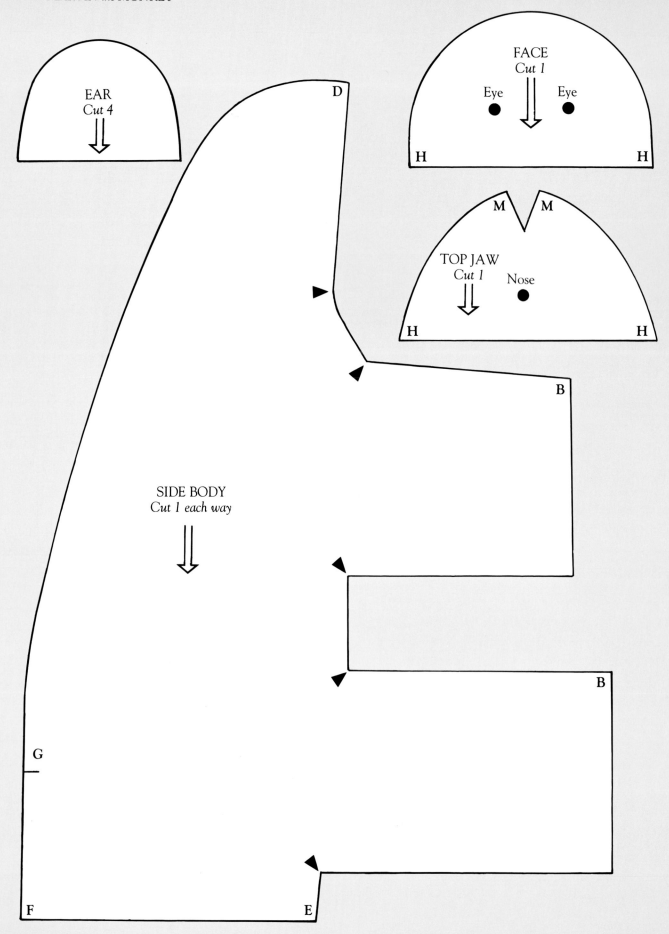

EAR
Cut 4

FACE
Cut 1

Eye Eye

H H

M M

TOP JAW
Cut 1 Nose

H H

D

B

SIDE BODY
Cut 1 each way

B

G

F E

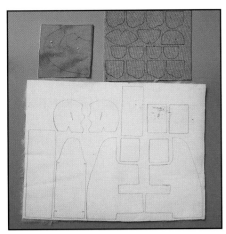

1 Make a pattern of each template
shape required (see p. 6). Then draw
around each pattern on the wrong side of
the appropriate material, as shown.

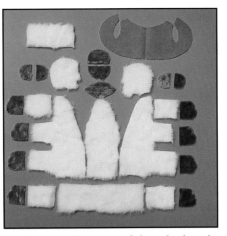

2 Cut out all pieces and then check with
the picture that all the sections are
there.

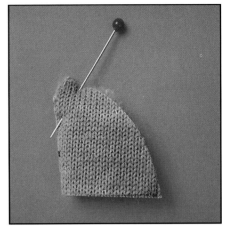

3 Pin **M** to **M** on top jaw, to form a
dart.

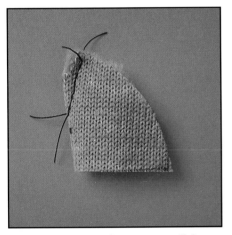

4 Stitch dart together tapering off the
ends. Open out to form the top jaw.

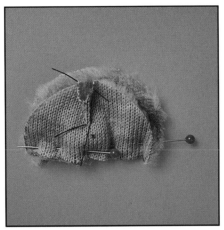

5 Pin top jaw to straight edge of face,
right sides facing, matching **H** to **H**.

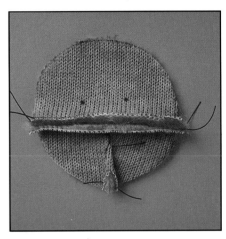

6 Stitch seam from **H** to **H**. Unfold
and brush seams.

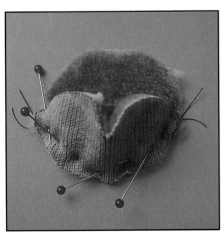

7 Pin lower jaw to top jaw, right sides
facing, from **H** to **H**.

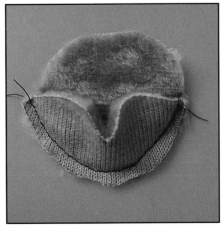

8 Stitch the seam from **H** to **H**, to
complete the face.

9 Turn the face right side out and brush
all seams.

10 Pin ear pieces together, right sides facing.

11 Stitch the pieces together leaving bottom edge open, as shown.

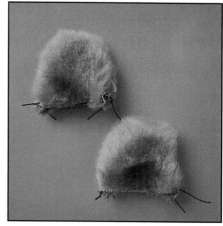

12 Turn each ear right side out and brush the seams.

13 Push an ear into a side head opening, leaving open end showing.

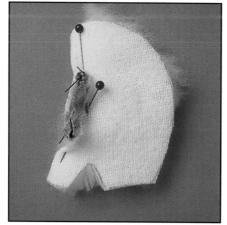

14 Fold the side head along the opening, right sides facing, and then pin together to secure the ear.

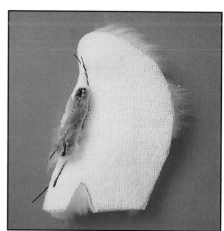

15 Carefully stitch into place, tapering off stitching as shown.

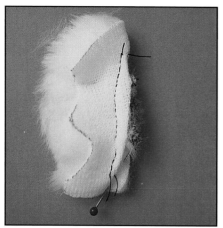

16 Pin dart together at position marked **N**.

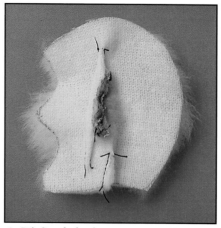

17 Stitch the dart, tapering off the seam. Repeat steps 13-17 for second side head.

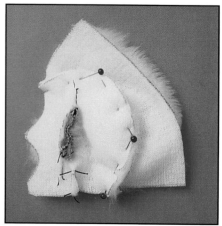

18 Pin side head to head gusset from **K** to **K**, as shown.

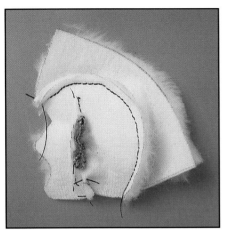

19 *Using seam allowance carefully stitch from **L** to **K**.*

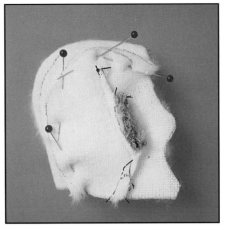

20 *Turn head over and then pin second side head to gusset from **K** to **L**.*

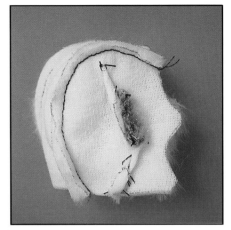

21 *Using seam allowance carefully stitch from **L** to **K**.*

22 *Place face into head, right sides facing, match and pin positions **J**, **H** and top centre of face.*

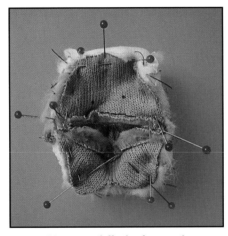

23 *Very carefully further pin face to head between the first pins, as shown.*

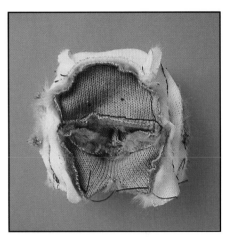

24 *Stitch face to head from **J** to **J**, leaving the neck open.*

25 *Place **J** to **J** on the lower jaw to form a dart, then pin in position.*

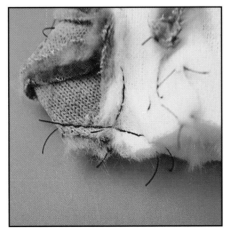

26 *Stitch the dart as shown. Insert safety eyes and nose. Turn right side out.*

27 *Brush head well. Stitch on a mouth (see p. 8) as shown. Stuff front of head firmly.*

28 Pin a paw to an arm, matching at **B**. Repeat for second arm.

29 Stitch along the seam line. Repeat steps 28-29 for legs.

30 Picture shows the arms and legs with paws correctly attached.

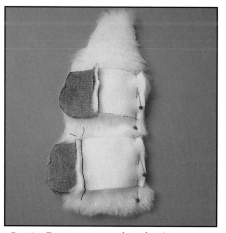

31 Pin an arm, right sides facing, at **A** on the front gusset. Then pin a leg at **C**.

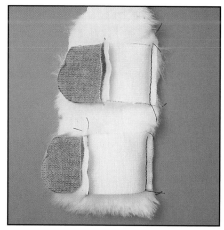

32 Stitch the arm and leg to the gusset as shown.

33 Repeat step 31 for the opposite arm and leg.

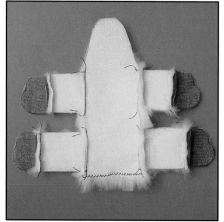

34 Stitch the arm and leg to gusset to complete the front. Turn up bottom edge and sew with zigzag stitch.

35 Pin paws to side body, right sides together, at **B**.

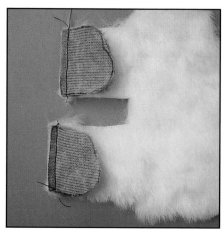

36 Stitch the paws into place. Repeat steps 35-36 for second side.

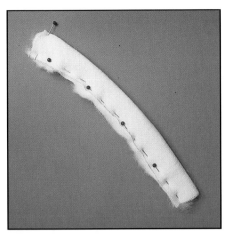

37 Fold tail in half, right sides facing, and pin along side and one end.

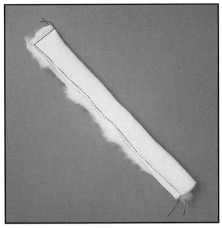

38 Using seam allowance stitch the tail, as shown.

39 Turn the tail right side out and brush the seam.

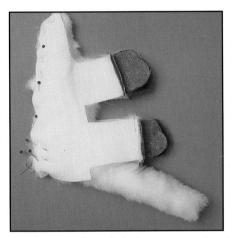

40 Pin tail to side body at position **G**. Place second side, right sides facing, to first and pin from **F** to **D**.

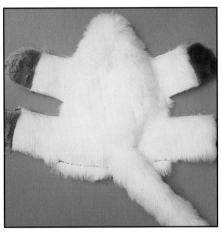

41 Stitch from **D** to **F**. Unfold body and turn up seam allowance, along bottom edge, and sew with zigzag stitch. Brush the seams.

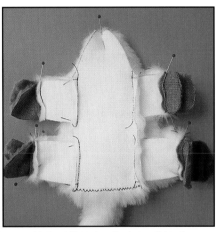

42 Place front on body, right sides facing, pin matching at positions **B** and **D**.

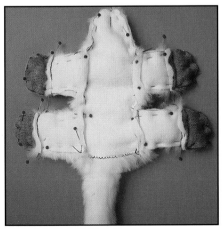

43 Continue pinning around body from **E** to **E**.

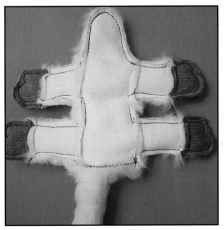

44 Carefully stitch body together from **E** to **E**, leaving bottom edge open.

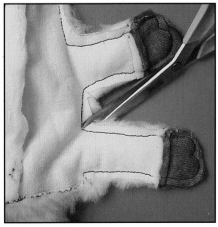

45 With sharp scissors, cut seam allowance to the stitching line at all ease points.

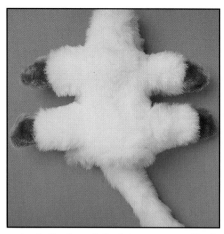

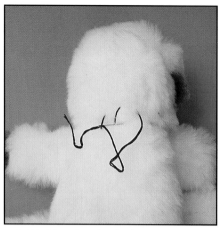

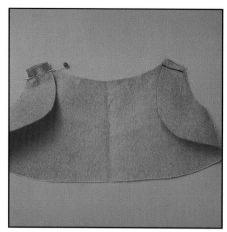

46 Push each limb into centre of body and turn right side out. Brush all over.

47 Place hand in body, insert neck into head. Pin and then sew head to neck. Secure the thread tightly.

48 Pin, then stitch, each shoulder seam on the jacket. Turn right side out and dress Marvin.

WRIGGLES *the* CATERPILLAR ☆☆☆

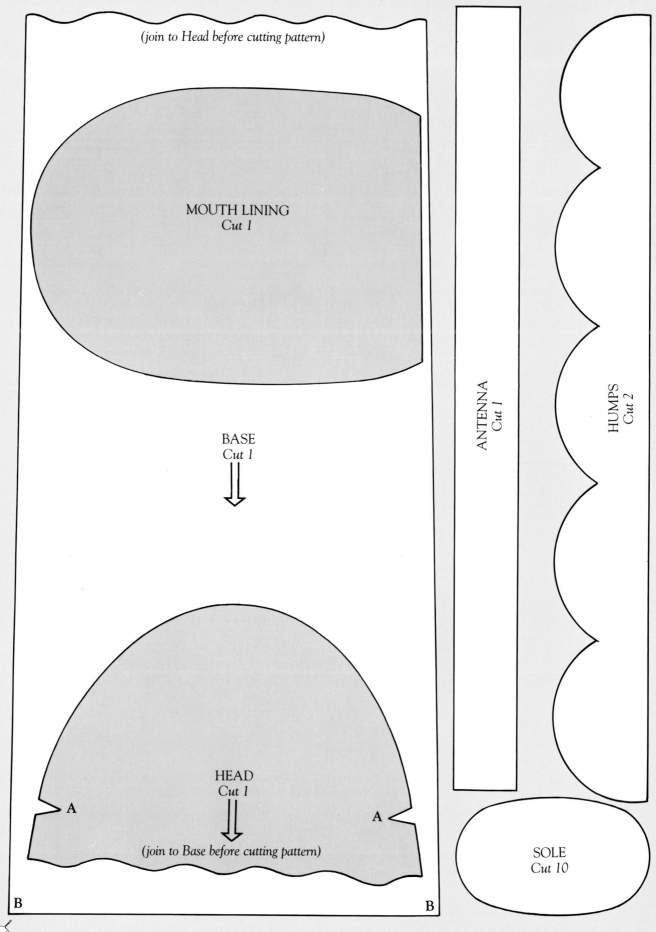

(join to Head before cutting pattern)

MOUTH LINING
Cut 1

BASE
Cut 1

ANTENNA
Cut 1

HUMPS
Cut 2

HEAD
Cut 1

A   A

(join to Base before cutting pattern)

B   B

SOLE
Cut 10

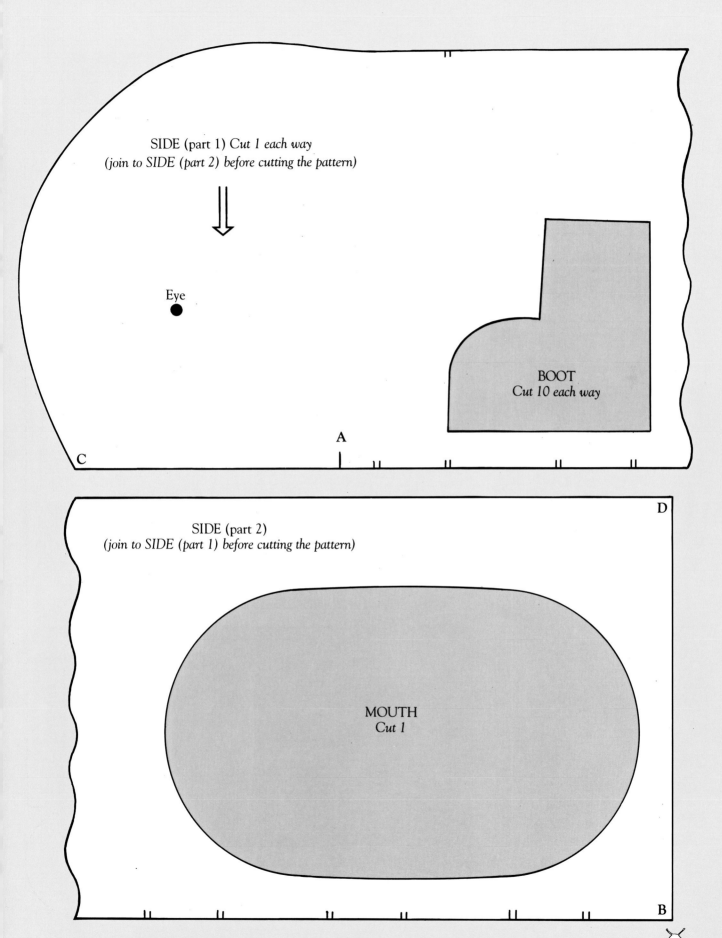

SIDE (part 1) *Cut 1 each way*
(join to SIDE (part 2) before cutting the pattern)

Eye

BOOT
Cut 10 each way

C

A

SIDE (part 2)
(join to SIDE (part 1) before cutting the pattern)

D

MOUTH
Cut 1

B

67

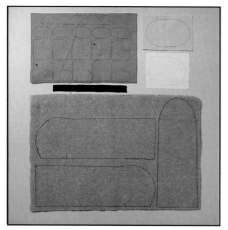

1 Make a pattern of each template shape required (see p.6). Then draw around each pattern on the wrong side of the appropriate material as shown.

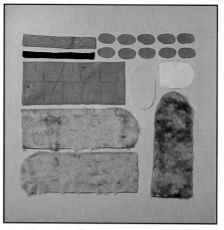

2 Cut out all pieces and then check with the picture that all the sections are there.

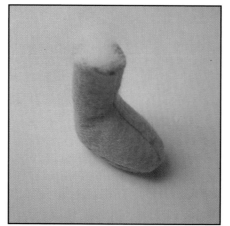

3 Pin a pair of felt feet together.

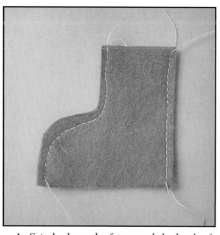

4 Stitch along the front and the back of the foot as shown.

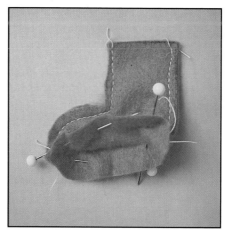

5 Open out bottom of foot and pin a felt sole to the base.

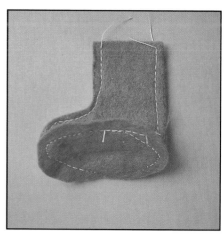

6 Stitch together to form the base of the foot.

7 Carefully turn foot right side out.

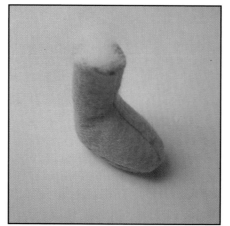

8 Fill with sufficient stuffing to make firm. Repeat steps 3-8 for the remaining nine feet.

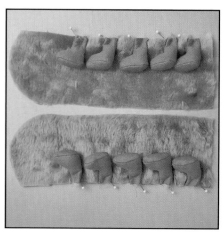

9 Pin five feet to each side body, at positions marked on the template.

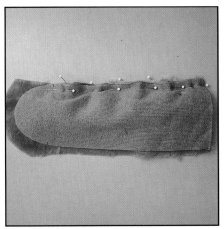

10 *Pin base to a side body, with right sides facing, from **A** to **B**.*

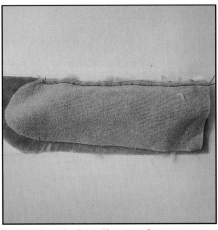

11 *Stitch along the top edge to secure feet.*

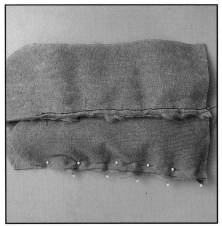

12 *Unfold with right sides facing, pin second side to base.*

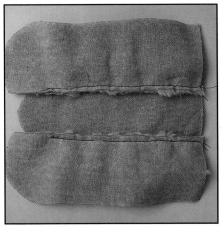

13 *Stitch along the bottom edge to secure feet, then unfold wrong side up.*

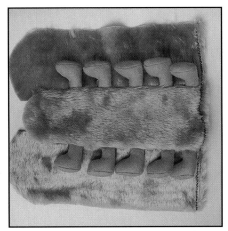

14 *Turn up the bottom edge and sew into place with zigzag stitch. Turn right side up and brush all seams, avoiding the felt feet.*

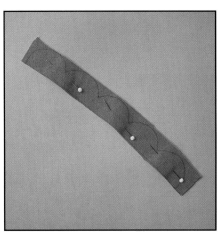

15 *Pin the humps together, as shown.*

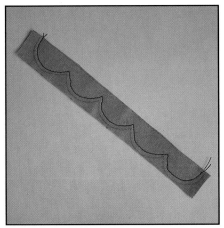

16 *Stitch beside the marked cutting line as shown.*

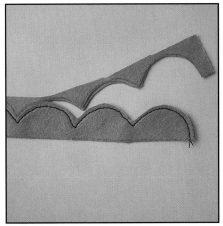

17 *Carefully cut the felt along the marked line.*

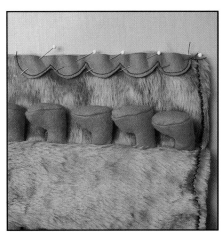

18 *Pin humps to the top edge of the side body in the position shown.*

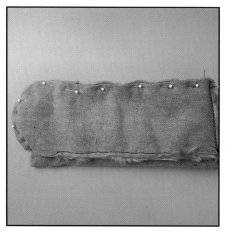

19 *Fold in half, right sides facing, and pin along front and top edge, from C to D.*

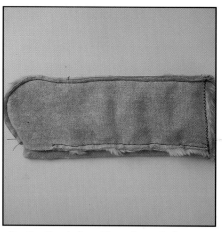

20 *Stitch from D to C, including the humps in the seam line, as shown.*

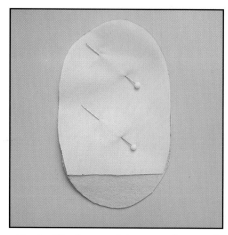

21 *Pin the mouth lining to the mouth, as shown.*

22 *Open top of body, then place and pin the mouth in position.*

23 *Stitch the mouth carefully to the body.*

24 *Slide the squeaker into the mouth lining and push it to the very top. Sew across the centre of the mouth to secure the squeaker.*

25 *Insert the safety eyes and then the nose, turn right side out.*

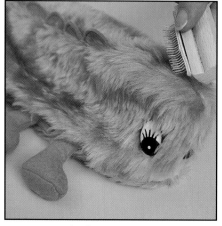

26 *Brush all seams, avoid brushing the felt.*

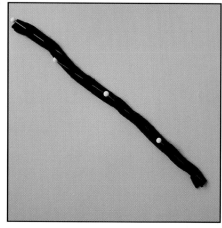

27 *Fold antenna lengthways and pin together.*

28 *Sew the antenna sides together, using a zigzag stitch.*

29 *Tie a knot at each end of the antenna and trim off the surplus.*

30 *Secure antenna to top centre of head, using a strong thread.*

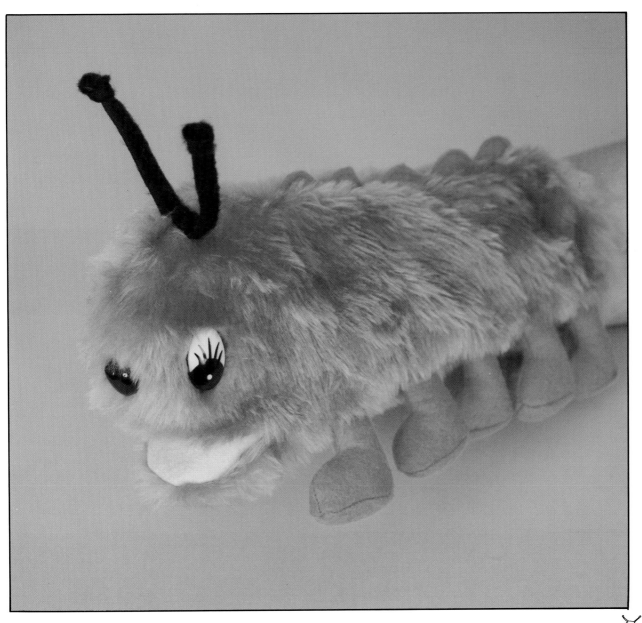

SPOT *the* DALMATIAN ☆☆

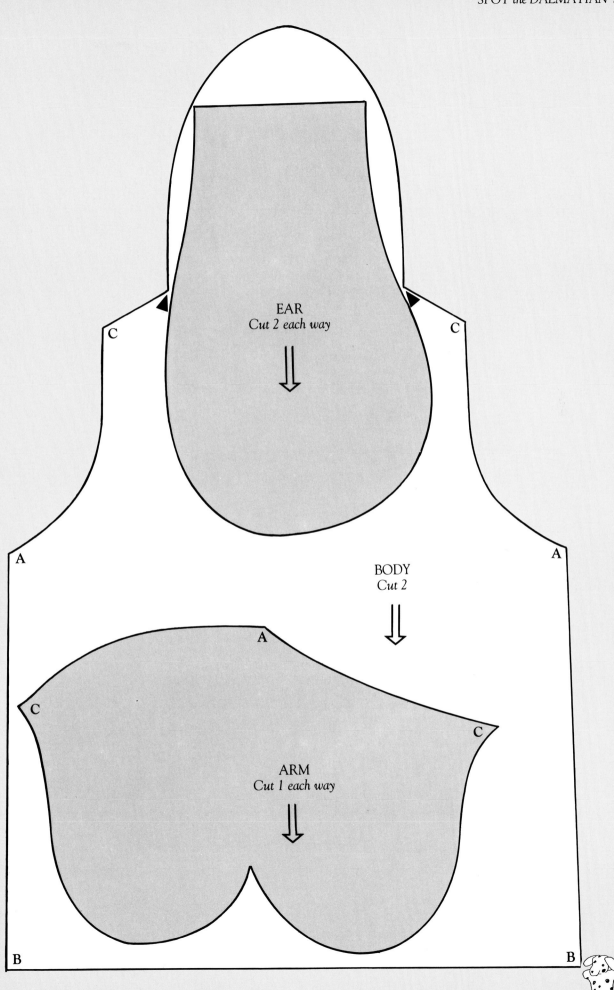

EAR
Cut 2 each way

C   C

A   A

BODY
Cut 2

A

C

C

ARM
Cut 1 each way

B   B

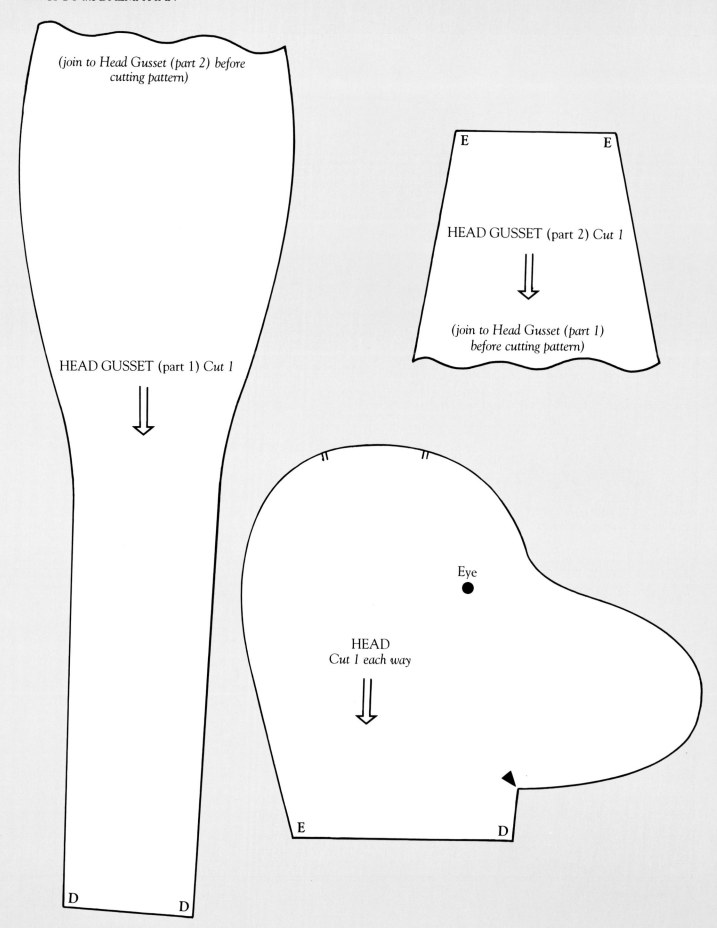

(join to Head Gusset (part 2) before
cutting pattern)

HEAD GUSSET (part 1) Cut 1

⇓

E   E

HEAD GUSSET (part 2) Cut 1

⇓

(join to Head Gusset (part 1)
before cutting pattern)

Eye

HEAD
Cut 1 each way

⇓

E   D

D   D

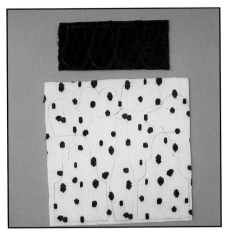

1 Make a pattern of each template shape required (see p.6). Then draw around each pattern on the wrong side of the appropriate material as shown.

2 Cut out all pieces and then check with the picture that all the sections are there.

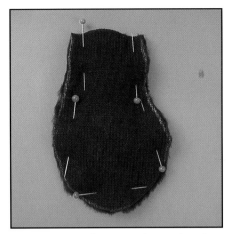

3 Pin a pair of ears together, right sides facing, leaving short side open.

4 Stitch around ears as shown leaving top open.

5 Turn right side out using the blunt end of a pencil. Brush seam.

6 Pin ear to top of head as shown. Repeat steps 3-6 for second side.

7 Pin head gusset to head, right sides facing, from **E** to **D**.

8 Carefully stitch gusset to head.

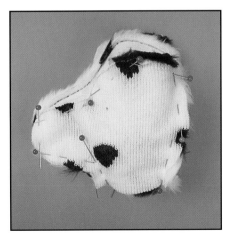

9 Pin second side to head gusset, right sides facing, from **D** to **E**. Leave neck open.

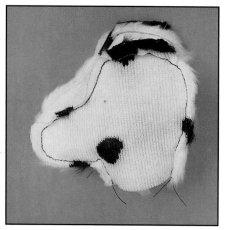

10 Stitch from **E** to **D** as shown. Insert eyes (see p. 8).

11 Carefully turn head right side out. Brush all seams. Insert nose (see p. 8).

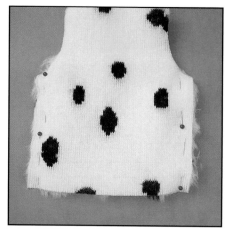

12 Position body sides together, right sides facing, and pin from **A** to **B** on both sides.

13 Stitch along each side from **B** to **A** as shown.

14 Fold back top half of body and pin on arm, matching at **C**, **A** and **C**. Repeat for second arm.

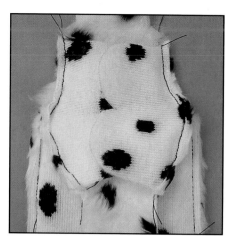

15 Stitch arms to body carefully as shown.

16 Open arms out. Refold puppet and pin from the top of the arms to **C**, over the top to second **C**, then to the top of the arm.

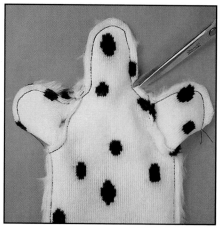

17 Stitch from arm to arm following the stitching line across the top. Cut at ease points as shown.

18 Turn right side out and brush all seams. Using the seam allowance, neaten the bottom with zigzag stitch.

19 *Stuff the muzzle and front of head firmly to fill out the face.*

20 *Place hand in puppet, slide head over top of body positioning as required.*

21 *Pin head in place and, using seam allowance, sew head to body firmly with ladder stitch.*

OLGA the OCTOPUS☆

MATERIALS

○ Green Polished Fur 330mm (13″) × 300mm (12″).

○ Yellow Polished Fur 205mm (8″) × 250mm (10″).

○ 2 Large Eyes.

○ Ribbon for neck.

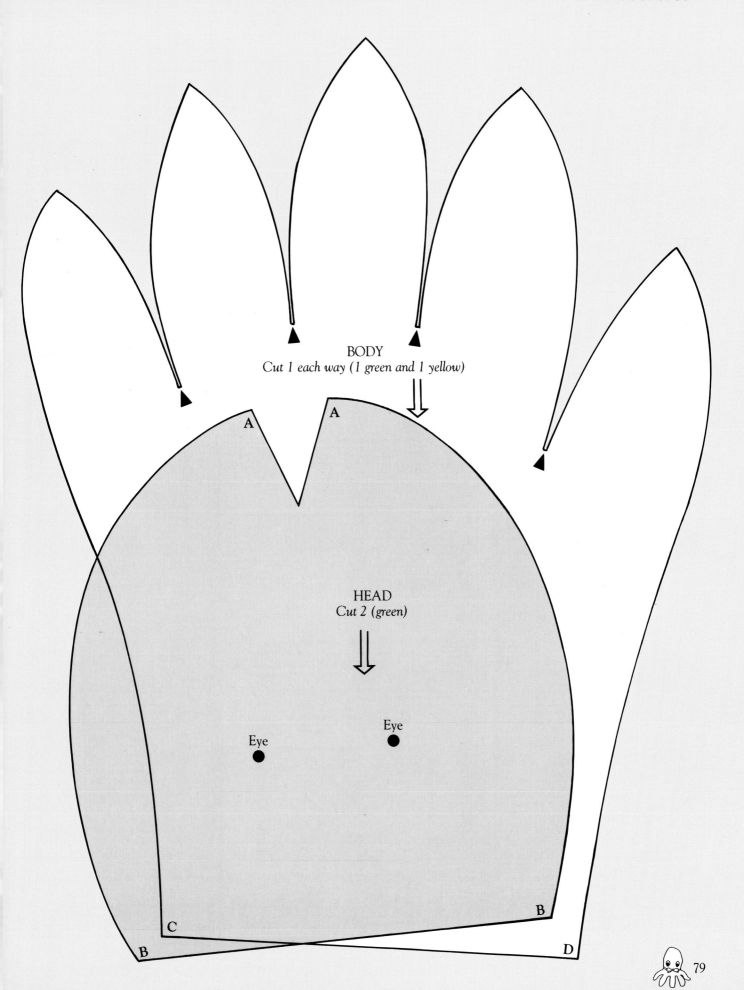

BODY
Cut 1 each way (1 green and 1 yellow)

A   A

HEAD
Cut 2 (green)

Eye   Eye

C

B   B   D

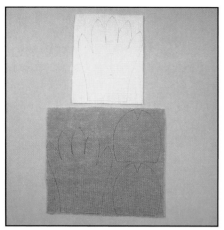

1 Make a pattern of each template shape required (see p. 6). Then draw around each pattern on the wrong side of the appropriate material as shown.

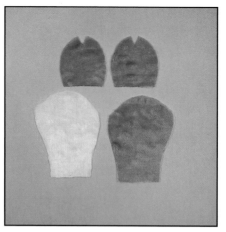

2 Cut out all pieces and then check with the picture that all the sections are there.

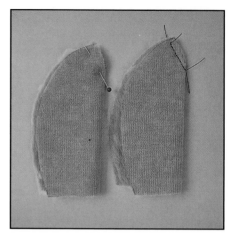

3 Pin, then stitch, a dart in each head piece, in position marked **A**.

4 Open the head pieces out and with right sides facing, pin together from **B** to **B**.

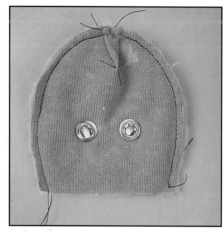

5 Stitch from **B** to **B**, leaving the bottom edge open. Insert eyes (see p. 8).

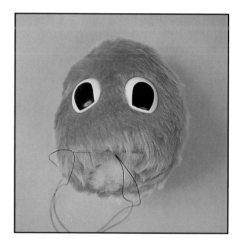

6 Sew a running thread around the head opening, then stuff firmly with filling. Pull up the thread slightly and secure.

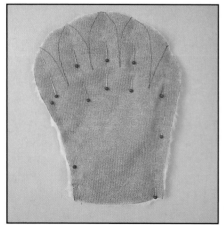

7 Place and pin body pieces together, right sides facing, as shown.

8 Stitch from **C** and, following inside the marked line (out-lining tentacles), finish at **D**. Cut to remove material between tentacles as shown.

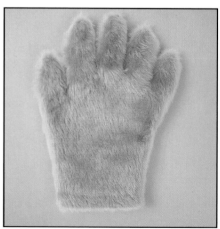

9 Carefully turn right side out and brush all seams.

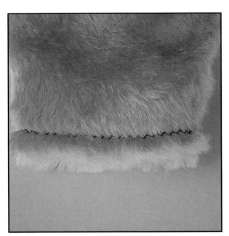

10 Turn up bottom edge and neaten with a zigzag stitch.

11 Place head on body and pin in chosen position. Stitch on firmly with strong thread.

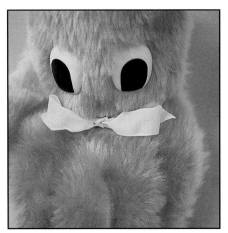

12 Tie ribbon around neck with double knot and bow.

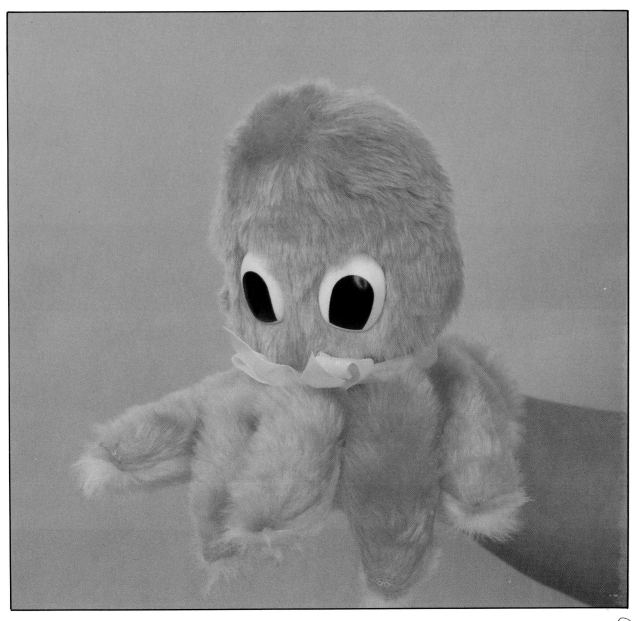

JACK *the* RABBIT ☆☆☆

MATERIALS

○ White Fur 475mm (19″) × 350mm (14″).

○ Pink Fur 125mm (5″) × 125mm (5″).

○ Orange Felt 90mm (3½″) × 100mm (4″).

○ Green Felt 20mm (1″) × 20mm (1″).

○ 2 Medium Goo Goo Eyes.

○ 1 Black Nose.

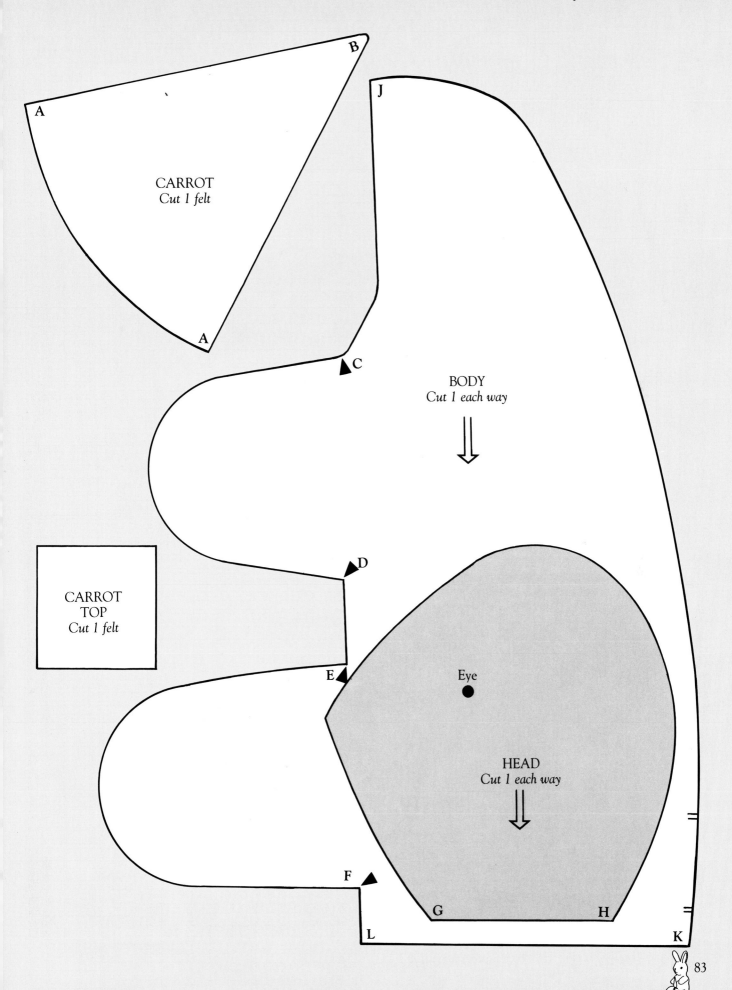

CARROT
Cut 1 felt

A

B

J

C

BODY
Cut 1 each way

⇓

CARROT
TOP
Cut 1 felt

D

E

Eye

HEAD
Cut 1 each way

⇓

F

G

H

L

K

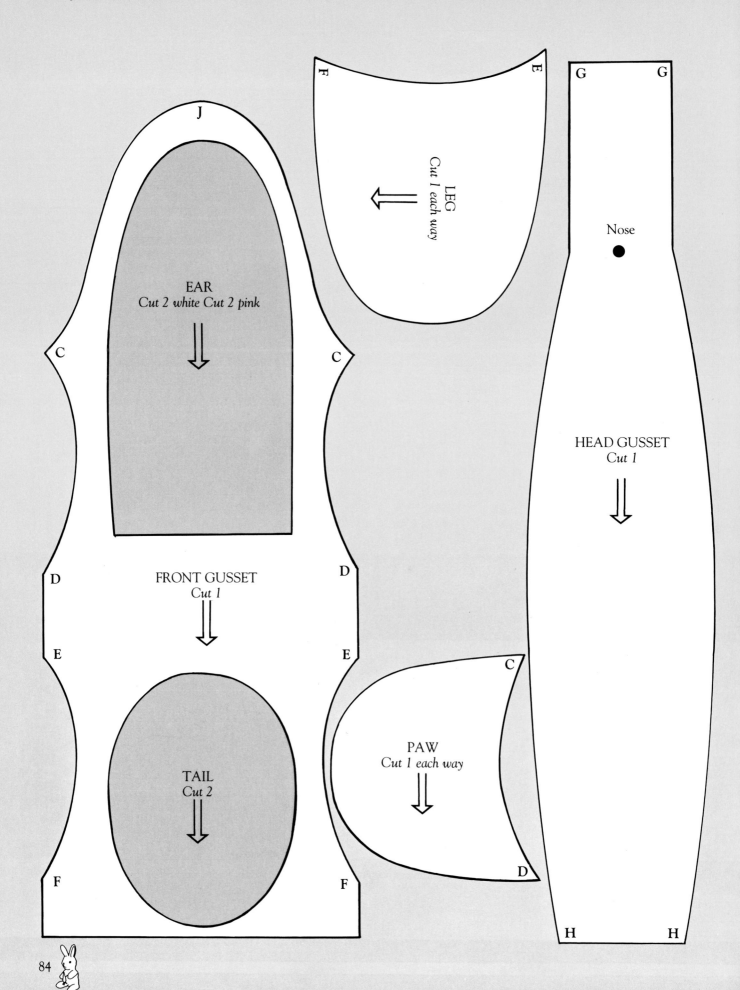

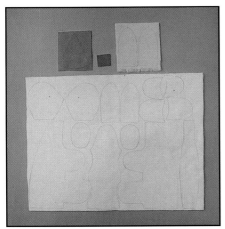

1 Make a pattern of each template shape required (see p.6). Then draw around each pattern on the wrong side of the appropriate material as shown.

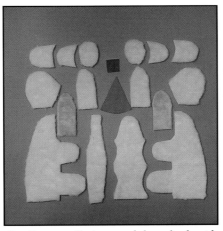

2 Cut out all pieces and then check with the picture that all the sections are there.

3 Pin inner ear to outer ear, right sides facing. Repeat for second ear.

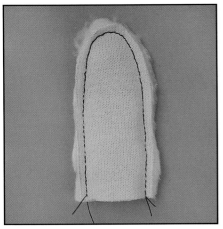

4 Stitch ears together along the outer edge, leaving bottom open.

5 Turn each ear right side out and brush seams. Fold and pin ears as shown.

6 Position an ear on each side head as shown. Pin in place.

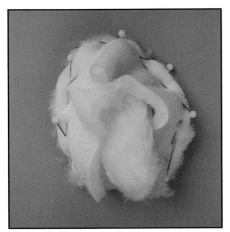

7 Pin head gusset to head, right sides together, matching at **G** and finishing at **H**.

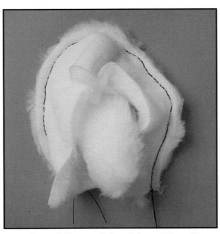

8 Carefully stitch head from **H** to **G**.

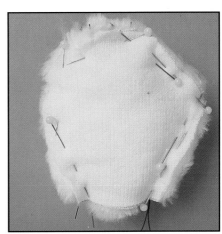

9 Place second head to gusset, right sides facing, and pin from **H** to **G**.

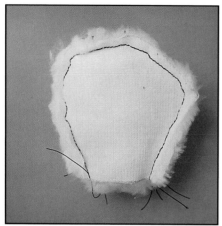

10 *Carefully stitch around head, leaving the neck open. Insert eyes (see p. 8).*

11 *Turn head right side out and brush all seams. Insert nose (see p. 8).*

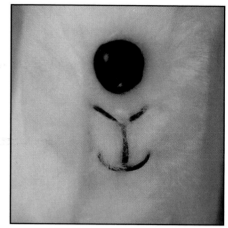

12 *Embroider bunny mouth with stranded cotton (see p. 9). Stuff front of head.*

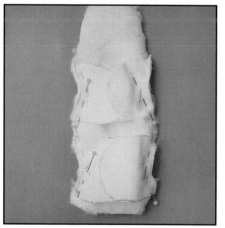

13 *Pin a leg to the front gusset, matching **F** and **E**, then a paw at **C** and **D**. Repeat for remaining leg and paw.*

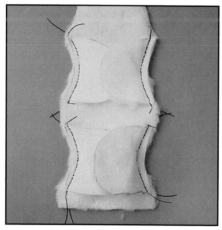

14 *Stitch legs and paws into place as shown following the stitching line. Unfold and brush all seams.*

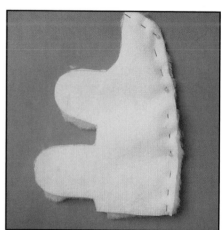

15 *Place body pieces together, right sides facing, and pin from **J** to **K**.*

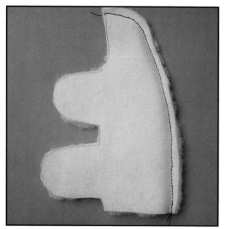

16 *Stitch body together. Unfold and brush seam.*

17 *Place front on back, right sides facing, and pin all round from **L** to **L** matching all marked positions.*

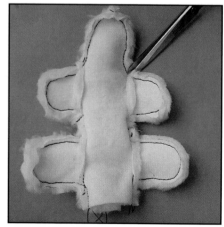

18 *Very carefully stitch round rabbit from **L** to **L** leaving base open. Cut all ease points.*

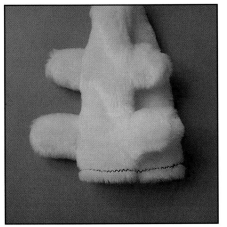

19 Carefully turn right side out and brush all seams. Using seam allowance, neaten opening with zigzag stitch.

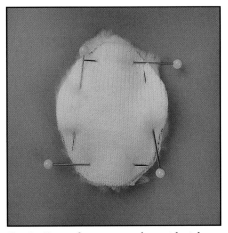

20 Pin tail pieces together with right sides facing.

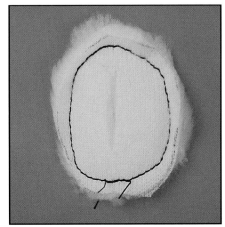

21 Stitch all round edge of tail. Cut a small opening in one side as shown.

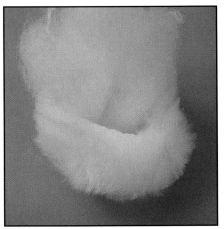

22 Turn tail right side out and brush seams. Stuff with a small amount of filling.

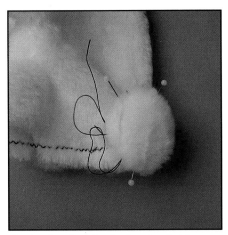

23 Stitch tail to body using ladder stitch and secure the thread.

24 Place hand in puppet, slide head over top of body positioning as required.

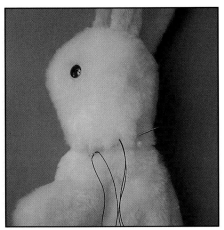

25 Pin head in place and, using seam allowance, sew head to body firmly.

26 Fold carrot in half, pin and stitch along the edge.

27 Turn right side out and pull into carrot shape.

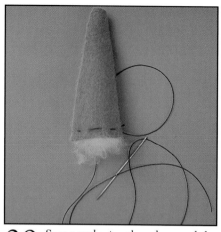

28 Roll up square of felt for carrot top and stitch one end. Cut to form fringe for the carrot top.

29 Sew a gathering thread around the base of the carrot. Stuff lightly, pull up thread and secure.

30 Stitch carrot top to the carrot. Shape carrot with a few stitches as shown. Stitch carrot to Jack's paw.

PATRICK the FOX☆☆☆

MATERIALS
○ Tan Long Fur 510mm (20″) × 385mm (15″).
○ Cream Polished Fur 125mm (5″) × 75mm (3″).
○ White Polished Fur 150mm (6″) × 100mm (4″).
○ 2 Medium Teddy Eyes.
○ 1 Animal Nose.

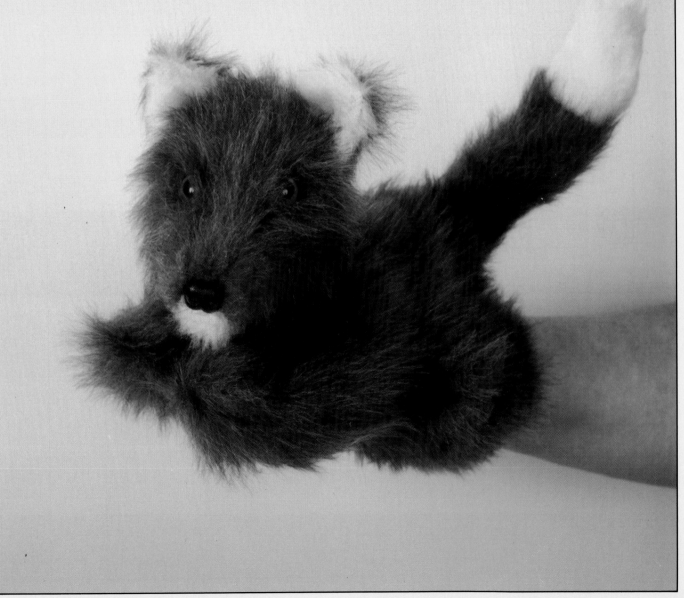

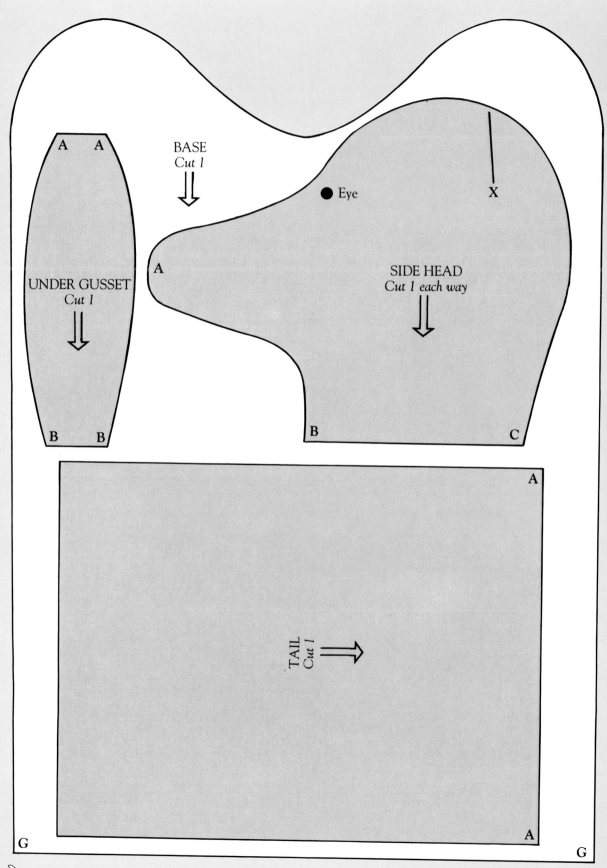

BASE
Cut 1

A A

UNDER GUSSET
Cut 1

A

B B

● Eye

X

SIDE HEAD
Cut 1 each way

B C

A

TAIL
Cut 1

G

A

G

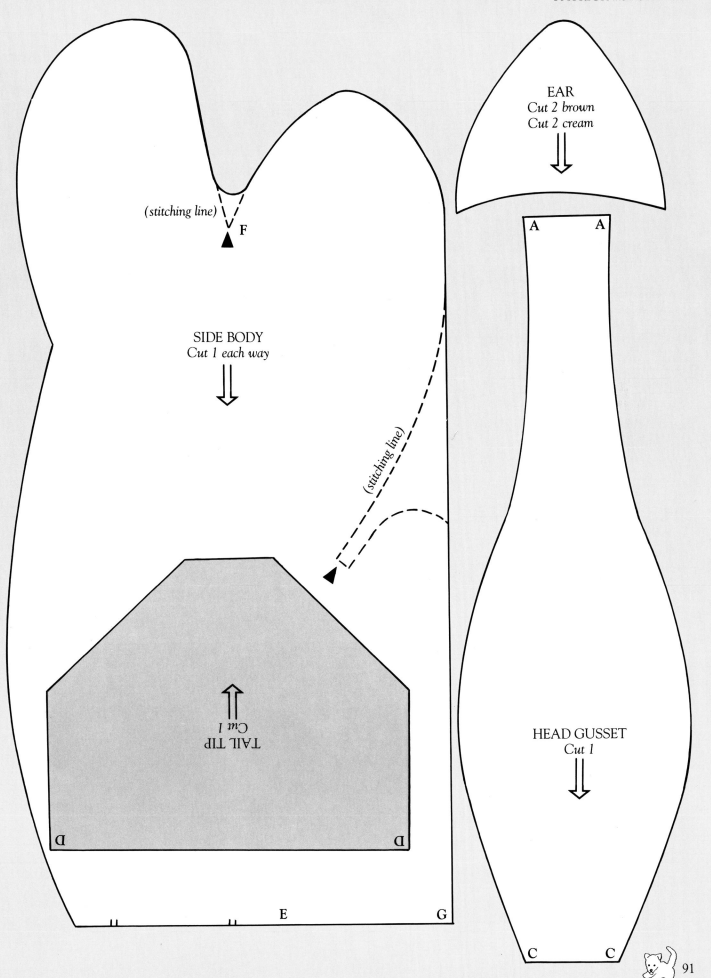

EAR
Cut 2 brown
Cut 2 cream

(stitching line)
▲ F

SIDE BODY
Cut 1 each way

(stitching line)

A   A

TAIL TIP
Cut 1

HEAD GUSSET
Cut 1

D   D

E   G

C   C

91

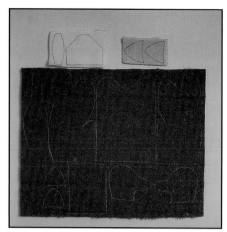

1 *Make a pattern of each template shape required (see p.6). Then draw around each pattern on the wrong side of the appropriate material, as shown.*

2 *Cut out all pieces and then check with the picture that all the sections are there.*

3 *Pin tail tip to tail, right sides facing, matching at* **D**.

4 *Stitch together and then unfold as shown. Brush seam.*

5 *Fold tail in half lengthways, then pin top and side edge together leaving bottom open.*

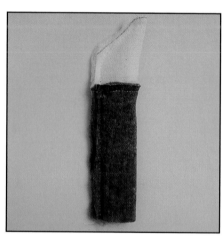

6 *Stitch the tail leaving bottom open.*

7 *Turn tail right side out and brush the seams.*

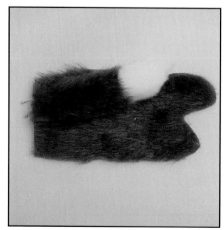

8 *Pin in position to side body.*

9 *Pin second side body to first from mark* **E** *to mark* **F**, *right sides facing.*

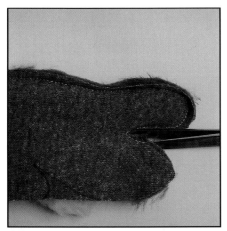

10 Stitch from mark **E** to mark **F**, then snip to seam line at **F**.

11 Open the body and place onto the base, right sides facing. Pin along the right side of the body from **G** to paw, following the stitching line.

12 Stitch together following the stitching line, from paw to **G**.

13 Open out body, turn up seam allowance and sew along bottom edge with zigzag stitch.

14 Refold the body, right sides facing and pin along the left side, following the stitching line.

15 Stitch from **G**, then under neck to paw. Snip at ease points, as shown.

16 Carefully turn right side out and brush all seams.

17 Pin each brown ear to each cream ear, right sides facing.

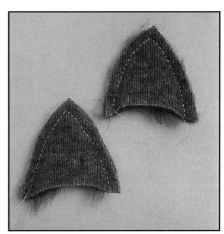

18 Stitch each ear together, leaving the bottom edges open.

19 Turn each ear right side out and brush seams.

20 Pin head gusset to under gusset at mark **A**, as shown.

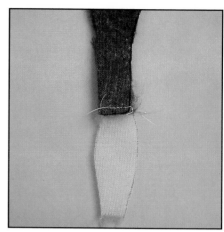

21 Stitch the two gussets together and then unfold.

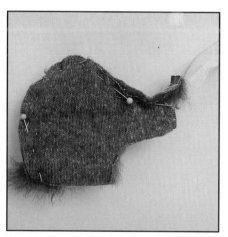

22 Pin side head to gusset, from **C**, to **A** then to **B**, right sides facing. Then stitch together.

23 Pin and stitch second side head to gusset, right sides facing, from **B** to **C**. Leave the bottom edge open.

24 Starting at mark **X** on side head, carefully cut ear opening across top of head gusset and down to mark **X** on second side head.

25 Insert ears into ear opening and pin from **X** to **X**.

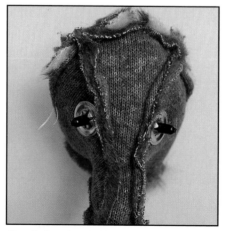

26 Stitch into place, tapering off ends. Insert safety eyes (see p. 8).

27 Gently turn head right side out and insert the nose. Brush all seams.

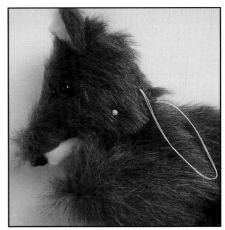

28 *Stuff the front of the head firmly to fill-out the face. Keep back of head free for fingers.*

29 *Place hand inside body and position head over neck, keeping the filling to the front.*

30 *Turn up seam allowance on head, pin and stitch into place. Brush all seams.*

Index